BUY THE RUMOR, SELL THE FACT

BUY THE RUMOR, SELL THE FACT

85 Maxims of Investing and What They Really Mean

Michael Maiello

McGraw-Hill

New York   Chicago   San Francisco   Lisbon
London   Madrid   Mexico City   Milan   New Delhi
San Juan   Seoul   Singapore   Sydney   Toronto

The McGraw·Hill Companies

1 2 3 4 5 6 7 8 9 0   AGM/AGM   0 9 8 7 6 5 4

ISBN 0-07-142795-3

McGraw-Hill books are available at special quantity discounts to use as premiums and sales promotions, or for use in corporate training programs. For more information, please write to the Director of Special Sales, McGraw-Hill Professional, Two Penn Plaza, New York, NY 10121-2298. Or contact your local bookstore.

 This book is printed on recycled, acid-free paper containing a minimum of 50% recycled, de-inked fiber.

Library of Congress Cataloging-in-Publication Data

Maiello, Michael, 1975-
    But the rumor, sell the fact : 85 maxims of investing and what they
    really mean / by Michael Maiello.
        p.   cm.
    ISBN 0-07-142795-3 (pbk. : alk. paper)
    1. Stocks. 2. Investments. I. Title.
    HG4661.M324   2004
    332.63'22—dc21

                          2003014705

Contents

Introduction

ALL OF THE UNCERTAINTY ABOUT THE FUTURE of social security and the shift from pension plans to stock market fueled 401(k) accounts has left Americans with the burden of knowing and playing the stock market, though many have little interest in the world of Wall Street. That forced entry into a confusing industry beset with institutional pitfalls and outright dishonesty leads to fear and to the desire for easy answers. But answers to the most important questions about when to enter the market and when to sell a favorite stock are always subjective. These myths attempt to remove subjectivity from the process, but they largely fail to do so.

They are important to know, however, because every investor who deals with a broker or financial adviser, or who consumes the financial press in its myriad forms, will be confronted with truisms designed to make the complex look easy and the risky look like a sure thing. The very existence of these myths sheds light on the psychology of the people who repeat them. Industry folk enjoy quoting Warren Buffett, saying that the ideal holding period for a stock is "forever." That's nice. But it isn't useful to the average person who's trying to plan a retirement or send a child to college on the strength of an investment portfolio. Stockbrokers might follow up a hot tip with the advice that you should "buy on rumor and sell on news." Again, that's nice. But which rumors? And what if they never make the news? I fear, and I think it will come through in the following discussions of various stock market myths and Wall Street wisdoms, that tired investment professionals often invoke these old saws in an attempt to set their clients' minds at ease and to get them out the door or off the phone before five o'clock.

Investors believe these notions because they desperately want to believe in something. The U.S. stock market is more than 200 years old, founded by 24 traders under a buttonwood tree in lower Manhattan in 1792. In the centuries that have passed since the creation of the New York Stock

Exchange, it seems likely that investors would have learned a few foolproof secrets to making money. But it isn't so and it can never be so. Investors make money by being right when the rest of the world is wrong. If an aphoristic phrase could pinpoint those moments in one or two easily memorized sentences, then everyone would know how to make money in every instance, and if they are rational, they will act on that knowledge. In that case, a clever investor could never beat the market. There would be no such thing, even as a clever investor. But we know that some investors have outperformed the markets, sometimes for decades. That means, in the very least, that none of these myths will work every time and that the best they can do is work more often than not. There's no such thing as a rule that always works and no such thing as an investor who's always right to follow them.

So investors are left on their own to find those moments where all the smart money acts out of ignorance. In a sense, investors are like entrepreneurs. Wal-Mart founder Sam Walton introduced the concept of "big box" stores to the retail market, and he made a fortune by bucking the established trends of inventory management. Pierre Omidyar of eBay used the Web to create an online yard sale and thus outpaced Jeff Bezos' Amazon.com, which, while great, is hardly different than the paper-catalogue companies of old. The market values eBay at $30 billion and Amazon.com at just $13 billion. Most entrepreneurs, we know, fail to change the world. Most investors fail too.

The hard truth is that most investors will, at best, match the overall return of the stock market over a long period of time. A lot of investors will fall behind the indexes. Winning this game, while not impossible, is certainly difficult.

As always, when something is difficult (be it golf, dieting, or investing), smart people will be susceptible to dubious information that sounds good. John Pierpont Morgan used to hold séances so that he could consult with the spirits of yesteryear's investing stars. So don't let uncertainty bother you. If you are not getting your stock tips from a flickering candle in the darkened sitting room of a glowering Victorian townhouse, then you are already one step ahead of one of the game's greatest players.

This book should be most useful whenever a broker, friend, or talking head utters one of the phrases (or something close to it) and you want to know where you are being steered. Not all of these maxims are wrong. Some are great for day traders but terrible for long-term investors, while others are geared toward Wall Street workers who spend their days moving other people's money. All of them, even the best, should be dealt with skeptically, just like everything else you hear, see, or buy on Wall Street.

P A R T

1

Beliefs from the Street

THE **FOLLOWING MAXIMS** concern the most common questions that a stock market investor faces. Should you try to beat the market or just match its performance? When should money go in, and when should it be pulled to the sidelines? These are also some of the most oft-repeated myths in the land.

No One Can Beat the Market

Despite what many people will say, particularly folks in the index fund industry like Vanguard founder John Bogle, a do-it-yourself investor or money manager can beat the market, even over long periods of time. The problem is that beating the market is so difficult that most people shouldn't try. It's true that for long-term investment advice, you could do a lot worse than to park your money in a low-cost Vanguard index fund and not think about it more than once a quarter. But some mutual fund managers have proven that superior performance can be bought or mimicked.

Consider the legendary Peter Lynch, now retired but often seen on Fidelity commercials alongside Don Rickles. At the helm of Fidelity's Magellan Fund between 1977 and 1990, Lynch earned annualized 29 percent returns against 15 percent returns for the S&P 500. Since he retired undefeated, one could argue that the market would have caught up with Lynch had he stuck around. But, the values he left on the fund, followed by successor managers like Morris Smith, Jeffrey Vinik, and now Robert Stansky, have continued to pay off.

Since Vanguard started its [S&P] 500 Index Fund (the first of its kind) in 1976, it has returned 11.9 percent annually. Magellan has returned 19.4 percent a year in that time period. One in three funds around since 1976 have managed to consistently beat Vanguard's cheap and easy index. That still means the odds are against an investor who wants to try, but there are lessons to be learned from the masters who have succeeded.

The first lesson is that value investing works. Magellan, whose holdings have an average trailing price-to-earnings ratio of 20 on its portfolio, is the priciest fund in the bunch. The average stock in the Sequoia Fund, which has returned 17.8 percent average annual return since 1976, trades at 18.7 times earnings. The typical Davis New York Venture Fund holding trades at 16.5 times earnings, and its portfolio has earned 16.4 percent since 1976. The S&P 500, even in the depressed conditions of early 2003, traded at 28 times trailing 12-month earnings.

Like the index they strive to beat, small-cap stocks make up an insignif-icant portion of these portfolios. Just 3.2 percent of the $16 billion Davis portfolio has been invested in stocks with market capitalizations under $2 bil-lion. Magellan has just 0.4 percent of its $60 billion in such stocks and Sequoia has less than 2 percent of its $3.6 billion fund invested in companies worth less than $2 billion.

A final point of similarity for these value managers: They all admire Warren Buffett, who famously remarked that the proper holding period for an investment is "forever." The Davis New York Venture Fund, the most active of the trinity, and managed since 1995 by Christopher Davis, turned over 22 percent of its portfolio last year. William J. Ruane's Sequoia Fund turned over just 7 percent, and it only owns 18 separate securities.

Now, here's a problem: Old funds tend to close. (Magellan and Sequoia aren't taking money.) But a good value investor can beat the S&P for decades, and there are other managers out there. If you want to do it your-self, follow the example of the best by building a portfolio that trades at less than 20 times earnings, shows no more than 2.7 times book value, and has a dividend yield of at least 1.3 percent. That should lead you to good stocks you can hold onto for a long time.

Money Is Made from Single Positions and Kept with Diversity

This is the way stock investing works in our imaginations: One startling insight and the courage to risk it all leads to an instant fortune. This is known to some as "hitting a home run" and to the less sports-minded as an act of sheer brilliance.

People believe in that one good pick because it's celebrated both in the media and among friends swapping investment stories. Bill Gates is worth more than $60 billion because he founded Microsoft and because he owns a lot of Microsoft. Some of the richest people in the world started a company, guided it to prominence, and owned an awful lot of it along the way. Indeed, most of their net worth is paper net worth and just a reflection of the value of the companies they founded. If Bill Gates tried to suddenly turn all of his Microsoft stock into cash by selling shares on the open market, he certainly wouldn't get $60 billion. His decision to liquidate his holdings would probably seriously impair Microsoft's stock price.

Remember also that, for the most part, Gates didn't buy his Microsoft stock on the open market. His holdings were awarded to him in exchange for his services in creating and guiding his company. Bill Gates, who started his company in a garage in Albuquerque, New Mexico, is the classic example of the entrepreneur who became wealthy. Glancing through the annual Forbes 400 list of richest Americans will yield yet more tales of folks who became wealthy based on their concentrated holdings in one company—usually companies they founded.

This lifestyle is not for everyone. The entrepreneur's life is consumed by the businesses that they create. (There's usually more than one, and usually a string of flops.) Though it's tempting to want to "be your own boss," most people would prefer to work for someone else who has to worry about payroll taxes, administering retirement plans, and cutting vacations short because a typhoon in southeast Asia delayed shipment of some vital widget that threatens the entire enterprise. An employee can keep life and work separate. Entrepreneurs can't do that.

Another entrepreneur, second to Gates in terms of personal wealth, illustrates the value of diversified investing in the very structure of the company he controls. Sure, Warren Buffett is rich because he owns a lot of Berkshire Hathaway, but Buffett's $30 billion net worth really arises from his decision to use Berkshire Hathaway to build a diverse stake of equity holdings that spans from Coca-Cola to the Mid-American Energy Company. Recently, Buffett even added junk bonds to his company's growing list of investments.

Most investors simply aren't home-run hitters. In the May 2002 issue of the *Journal of Financial Planning,* Mark Riepe of the Schwab Center for Investment Research tried to test how hard it is to hit a home run. He set up a computer program that, from January 1926 through December 1997 randomly purchased a stock every day and then tracked the return for one year against the market. He ran the program 75,000 times and found that, not surprisingly, the biggest winners won by huge margins but that they are rare. In the large-cap sector, 97.5 percent of the random picks produced losses worse than 50 percent. But 2.5 percent of those picks produced gains greater than 90 percent. In the mid-cap and small-cap sectors, 97.5 percent of the random picks lost more than 80 percent while 2.5 percent of them gained more than 150 percent.

Also, make no mistake, real wealth measured in millions of dollars arises from owning a lot of stock: A holder of a stock trading at $50 a share needs to own 100,000 shares to have a $5 million position. An already wealthy investor might be able to amass a large position in a company that will yet grow larger, but most investors aren't threatening to take over board seats when they tell their brokers to establish a position. The average investor trying to become rich is best served by creating a diversified portfolio that can be monitored and occasionally retooled over the course of decades. In that way, stock splits, price appreciation, and the miracle of compounding returns will create wealth with relatively little risk.

If you're one of the lucky few who did get rich off a home-run pick, don't be afraid to diversify. The point to owning a lot of stocks is that they won't all be going up or down at the same time. On the upside, that means that the losers will eat into the overall return a bit. On the downside, the winners will help to prevent catastrophic loss. Sometimes the market will rule and even a well-diversified portfolio will move entirely in one direction or the other. But watch the financial report on the evening news on a day-to-day basis and you will constantly hear statements like "winners beat losers today by 3 to 2," meaning that three stocks went up for every two that declined. Rarely, if ever, will you hear that "every stock went up." That variety of individual stock performance is why diversification works.

It's tempting to want to stick with a stock that's paid off so well, but excessive exposure to one stock is always risky. Every year, people fall off of the Forbes 400, usually due to price swings on their major holdings. Martha Stewart, for example, was on the list in 2001 and then off it in 2002 after Martha Stewart Living Omnimedia lost 60 percent of its value. She's no pauper, of course, but she might have protected her wealth through diversification.

As for the myth at hand, it's true that concentrated positions sometimes make people wealthy. But either luck, exceptional skill, or special circumstances (being a company founder or an already wealthy investor) makes that happen, while diversification is still a proven tool for creating and preserving wealth in the long term.

Don't Average Down on a Loser

"Averaging" means investing a fixed amount of money in a particular stock, over a set course of time. "Averaging down" means that the investor has specifically chosen a period of time when a stock's price is in decline. It's a tool that can be useful to value investors and bottom feeders who like to buy stocks that are out of favor. But it is rather controversial because there's always a chance that a stock is getting hammered for a reason. Obviously, an investor who wants to buy a stock as it drops, in the hopes of accumulating more shares for less money and to participate in a later upswing, has got to know the company at hand extremely well. This is a classic bet against the rest of the market, and the market is always a formidable foe.

Woody Allen tells a joke in *Annie Hall*: Two women are in a restaurant and one says to the other, "The food here is terrible." The other woman agrees, "Yes, and such small portions." Stock investors are often in the business of trying to buy plentiful quantities of terribly cooked food in the hopes that the flavor will improve with age. Value investors who look to buy stocks with low price-to-earnings ratios, or low price-to-book ratios, will often see opportunities in stocks that are being priced under duress. The cheaper the price, after all, the cheaper it is to buy a piece of that company's earnings or assets. If a company trading at $20 and 11 times earnings looks like a good value, then it should represent an even better value at $13 and 7 times earnings.

Hardened investors know, of course, that sometimes stocks don't stop falling until they roll over and die. A saying that often accompanies "don't average down on a loser" is "don't throw good money after bad." It's important to be confident that the market is wrong and that whatever bad news is depressing the stock is either overblown or temporary. This problem isn't unique to the investor who's averaging down. Any investor who holds a stock in decline, or who makes a single purchase of a stock in decline, has to worry about having made the wrong call.

There are also return-diminishing costs to investing this way. Every time an investor adds money, there's a brokerage fee to be paid. A $500 investment might cost $15, meaning that the stock will have to appreciate by 3 percent just to pay for the costs of buying it. Now look at the investor who's averaging down: $100 invested weekly over a month would cost $60, meaning that the investment is down 12 percent after the first month, in addition to any losses incurred by the stock. That puts a lot of pressure on the stock's future performance. The fees don't cut so heavily into return for investors with larger sums of money, and they don't matter at all for investors who play a flat, yearly fee for unlimited trades. The small investor who pays for every trade should be extremely fee-conscious and very careful when implementing this strategy.

Cut Your Losses and Let Your Profits Run

For an investment portfolio to make money over time, the bad picks can't lose more than the good picks gain. That means that investors have to limit losses by selling while making sure that the best choices have enough time to provide adequate return. It sounds simple, but a lot of investors do the opposite by selling their winners in order to take profits and holding onto the losers in the hopes of a rebound. The inevitable result to that strategy is a portfolio full of cash and losers.

Todd Salamone, vice president of research at Schaeffer's Investments, cautions investors that "you've got to be conscious about your expected win rate." Among professional traders and mutual fund managers, says Salamone, the best returns come from a few good picks and a willingness to admit a mistake in the face of those that don't pan out. Most investors have a win rate of less than 50 percent, meaning that more than half of their picks lose money.

The key, then, is not to let those picks lose too much. "If you have a win rate of less than 50 percent, it's essential for your average win to exceed your average loss," says Salamone. To figure out how much bad news your portfolio can bear, take your average win and multiply it by your win rate, then subtract your average loss and multiply that by your loss rate.

For example, an investor with a 40 percent win rate whose average good pick returns 70 percent and whose losers drop 35 percent would make only 7 cents on every dollar invested:

$$0.4 \text{ (win rate)} \times 0.7 \text{ (avg. win)} = 0.28$$
$$0.6 \text{ (loss rate)} \times 0.35 \text{ (avg. loss)} = 0.21$$
$$0.28 - 0.21 = \$0.07$$

Obviously, 70 percent gains on good picks is nothing to count on, and with a profit margin so slim, our hypothetical investor is going to have to cut losses earlier in order to boost returns.

For long-term stock investing, Salamone expects a 10 percent return per year, if he holds stocks for an average of five years. "I understand that every time I buy a stock for five years I'm right about 45 percent of the time," he says. So I know my average win has to exceed my average loss by more than 2 to 1."

It takes a while for investors to figure out what their win rate is and, of course, it's going to improve with experience. So there's some homework to be done in analyzing past trades and looking for year-to-year patterns. New investors can practice by trading on paper and creating a hypothetical portfolio to see where their stock-picking skills are.

The selling might be difficult, of course, since some investors see it as an admission of failure. There's also a good case to be made for holding on to stocks that have fallen on rough times, if there's some fundamental reason to believe that they will bounce back. It's also a bad idea to overtrade the portfolio, because brokerage fees add up. But remember, there are virtues in selling losers. The capital losses on the not-so-good picks can eliminate capital gains on the picks that went well.

If Investments Are Keeping You Awake at Night, Sell Down to the Sleeping Point

This little nugget is more psychological advice to the investor than it is predictive of the market, but financial advisers are often in the business of telling clients how they should feel in addition to telling them what to do. Investing is an intellectual activity with uncertain outcomes, and it's important for investors to master their emotions in order to make rational choices. Obviously, a notion like this can't be measured quantitatively, but it has still been uttered over and over again by weary brokers fielding panicked calls at the end of the trading day. It's easy to see why such a phrase would be popular among that crowd, and it has the benefit of playing to that distinctly American notion of trusting your gut.

But before you trust that gut, you have to figure out how well informed your gut is. The 1990s gave investors a gift with a curse attached because a lot of people got it into their heads that investing is easy. That's a good thing, because it encouraged individuals to enter the market. That's one of the only ways that the modern American worker will be able to earn sufficient returns for retirement, especially with fixed-benefit pension plans (as well as sticking to one job for decades) becoming more and more rare. But it's a curse because stock investing isn't easy. Some people devote years of study and debt to expensive graduate schools just to learn how to do it, and then they continue paying dues at some fairly low-paying Wall Street jobs until they get called up to the big time. That's not to say you can't learn to do it yourself; you can and you should. But it isn't as easy as trusting your gut.

Selling to the sleeping point basically means panic selling. It's much better to have diversified investments and a long-term goal that you can sleep with than it is to make portfolio adjustments based on anxiety. Remember that one of the tragedies of Enron was that employees who had put most of their retirement savings in company stock were left with nothing. Their guts didn't warn them. So the gut is fallible.

Remember also that if you're trying to beat the market, then you are basically trying to be right while other people are wrong. That's a very difficult position to be in. We have all known people who will strongly express an opinion about a movie, restaurant, or band who will, when confronted with the opposite opinion, backtrack entirely. We have probably all been that person. No matter how individualistic we are, we also crave the comfort of solidarity with people around us.

But we also know that millions of investors can be wrong. Hence, the 1990s. It's easy to sleep on a growing portfolio of technology stocks, at least for a while.

I won't go so far as to say that you should be dispassionate or that you shouldn't trust your intuition when making investments. If you can't sleep because you don't like owning tobacco stocks or weapons manufacturers, then by all means sell. But when you've made an intellectual decision to buy an out-of-favor stock that you think has unrealized value, then you are probably going to lose sleep a few times.

Of course, never invest more in such stocks than you can afford to lose. But don't invest with the goal of feeling comfortable either. There is risk in the stock market. The risk diminishes with time and diversification so that it becomes a bearable risk.

But so long as you are diversified and you have a decent time horizon, then you can also go against the grain with some of your stock selections and you can take a reasoned, well-thought-out risk on an out-of-favor stock. The key then is to ignore those butterflies in your stomach and try to sleep on the investment, because time is the magic ingredient in value investing.

If you are buying or selling a stock because you can't sleep, then you need to step back and try to articulate a practical reason for your sale. If it's that you can't afford such a large investment in that stock, fine. If it's that the fundamentals have changed, fine. But if you're just spooked, then calm down.

Beware the Triple Witching Day

The Triple Witching Day is as mysterious as it sounds. On the third Friday of every month, equity and index options (securities that represent the right to buy or sell stocks at a given time and price) expire. The thinking goes that the major institutions that own these options all have to rebalance their portfolios or roll over their options at once, causing extreme volatility in the market. That's the Double Witching Day. On the third Friday of March, futures (the right to an equity or commodity at some future time) owned by these institutions expire as well and that's the Triple Witching Day.

The pattern isn't so clear says Jerry Wang, a quantitative analyst at Schaffer's Investment Research. For one thing, the effect, if felt at all, is temporary and has very little interest to the long-term stock investor. It only lasts a day or maybe for an afternoon. Folks who track this kind of thing do it on a minute-by-minute basis.

Wang studied trading patterns around the S&P 100 for 27 years. Since January 1976 he found that the average daily trading range is about 1 percent. On options' expiration day he also found the S&P 100 trading in 1 percent swings. On the Triple Witching Day it is also 1 percent. "Overall, the triple witching expirations have the same volatility as the average market day," he says.

Those are averages. When the data is broken down further, it shows an only slightly different picture. Between September 1983 and June 1995 the average daily range was 1.16 percent and the Triple Witching Day was 1.26 percent. Between July 1995 and June 2000, the Triple Witching Days were much less volatile, showing a 0.68 percent range, while the average remained 1.16 percent.

Only hour-to-hour day traders really have to worry about Triple Witching Day, even if the phenomenon were true; it is something that needn't concern anybody.

If You Wouldn't Buy a Stock at That Price, Sell It

Owning an overvalued security is nearly as dangerous as buying one, since both are doomed to eventual decline. One good way of determining whether or not stocks you have already bought are overvalued is to ask yourself if you'd buy it at the moment. If the answer is no, then it's reasonable to assume you'd have a hard time selling it at that price as well. Believing otherwise rests on the arrogant assumption that everyone else is a sucker.

This myth is particularly useful because it addresses one of the hardest investing questions: Should I sell? Buying a stock is akin to making a bet on a company's future. Once the future has arrived, an investor has to look even farther ahead to see if prospects still look bright. But, like all of the myths in this book, this one isn't a hard and fast rule. There are reasons for continuing to own a stock even if it doesn't represent the same kind of value it did back when it was purchased.

Stock selection takes hours of homework, but it doesn't end once an order is placed. The good news is that the average investor's portfolio is usually smaller than the entire stock market, so this kind of portfolio maintenance work takes less time and effort than stock selection does. Still, it's a good idea, a few times a year, for investors to comb through their portfolios, looking stock by stock, at past selections to make sure that they still represent reasonable purchases. In this way, stocks are unlike consumer purchases. DVD players aren't sold because cheaper models pop up on store shelves, and cars aren't sold because the dealer has decided to close out the model. Stocks, because of their constantly changing prices and usually abundant liquidity, have to be monitored periodically.

One obvious reason to sell a stock is that its price has appreciated at a much faster rate than its earnings, thus driving up its price/earnings (P/E) ratio. If you bought a stock at 11 times earnings, feeling that you'd paid a reasonable price, you might well decide to sell it if, at quarterly checkup, it's pushing 20 times earnings. Pretend that you don't own the stock and that your broker has just suggested buying in at 20 times earnings. Would you take his advice? If not, then get rid of it, because the stock has probably run out of upside. That doesn't mean that the stock is going to collapse tomorrow or even in the next few months. It might only mean that its period of rapid price growth is over and that its returns will be smaller going forward. That's all right, as there might be other companies within the sector that are still trading at low multiples and are ready to appreciate. It could be a good time to sell and to buy into a stock that represents greater value.

Of course, there are tax implications to the sale and commissions to be paid on the trade. There's nothing wrong with paying the 15 percent tax on capital gains. After all, investors should want to pay taxes because it goes hand in hand with making money. But if the return doesn't look attractive after taxes and trading fees, the stock might be worth hanging on to for a while longer.

Sometimes, as we saw recently with the technology and telecommunications industries, an entire sector might become overvalued. If that's the case, and you are unwilling to cut exposure to the sector completely, there might not be good, cheap alternatives to the overvalued stock in the portfolio. If both Coca-Cola and Pepsi are expensive, it doesn't make sense to trade one for the other; the real question becomes whether or not you should invest in soft drinks at all.

Occasionally, for the sake of diversification, an investor will stick with some exposure to a given sector even though valuations aren't favorable. That diversification will help a portfolio track the overall market's return. Since most portfolios only outperform the market on the basis of a few stock selections (take out the winners and you wind up with performance identical to the market's), that diversification keeps the portfolio from falling behind. It's admittedly a tough call, but it undermines the notion that you should in all circumstances sell stocks that you wouldn't buy.

In any event, the answer won't always come up "sell." Sometimes a value stock will remain a value stock even as its price appreciates. If the company's earnings grow as a stock gets more expensive, than the P/E multiple shouldn't change much. At that point, check out the future. If the business model is still solid and not about to be eroded by new competition and if analysts are forecasting solid earnings growth in the coming years, then it's probably a stock worth keeping. If the company has gained market share and is forecasting better earnings growth to come, then there's a chance that the stock is a better value now than it was when it was purchased.

The real value of this saying is that it forces investors to periodically examine their holdings when they are all too often purchased and forgotten. Stock selection is a lot of work, but so is portfolio maintenance. Neither job should be neglected.

Bull Markets Climb a Wall of Worry

View the market as an amalgam of different and sometimes competing minds and it makes sense that though the overall sentiment might lead toward one outcome, powerful forces can temporarily pull it in another. The "Wall of Worry" behind every bull market is the group of bearish investors who are either shorting equities or constantly selling to take profits and who can cause severe dips during a long bull run.

The market corrections of 1998 and 1999 provide a great example of how the Wall of Worry works. During this period, investors experienced dips in major indexes like the S&P 500, which fell from 1190 to 950 in the space of a month, well below its 20-month average. The Wall of Worry cautions that such dips aren't tantamount to the beginning of a bear market. In 1998 and 1999, the markets recovered. The bears that caused the sell-off might even be a reason for the recovery.

Think of it this way: There's only so much investable money in the world. If none of it is sitting on the sidelines, then the market can't go up any farther. Without the Wall of Worry, all investors would be fully invested (a result of nobody being worried about the market), and there would be no sideline money to drive prices higher. When the market is mostly full of optimists, a comparatively slight bit of selling pressure can temporarily cause a mild panic and downturn.

The theory is nothing, of course, without some fundamental backing, because the sidelined money has to want to move back into the market. The Asian and Russian financial crises were two valid reasons for investors to jump out of the stock market in 1998. What brought them back was that throughout 1999 companies continued to beat earnings and revenues estimates by between 10 and 20 percent.

The theory in this case also applies to individual stocks. For a stock to continue to climb in price, there must be ready buyers, waiting on the sidelines, who might be expressing skepticism. Watch the media and analysts. If no one is offering any caveats about a company, it's at the top of every analysts' rankings, and it's gone through a major price explosion over the last few months, then the stock is probably played out. Any investor who wanted to own it has already bought in. There should be a little worry, a little uncertainty, about a stock that still has room to move. One key to stock picking, after all, is to find good values that the rest of the market has neglected. If every analyst is behind a company and all the press is good, then it's just not a special find.

For both stocks and the markets, investors tend to build obstacles to whatever trend is in place. There's a lot of chatter among the traders, the common investor, and the institutions. Were everyone in agreement, the market would always be static. So, of course, the Wall of Worry exists during the good times, and the good times could never get better without it.

Bear Markets Slide Down a Slope of Hope

A corollary to the Wall of Worry—the "Slope of Hope"—represents all of those temporary and ephemeral market rallies that take place while the bears are ruling the market. It basically represents investors throwing good money into a bad market.

Remember the rhetoric of the recent bear market. Between March 2000 and March 2001, the media was abuzz with talk about an earnings recovery being right around the corner, or actually during the quarter. Always it was "the next quarter," or "a few quarters away." Fund managers on the financial talk shows referred to the market as the best buying opportunity in years. Meanwhile, the S&P 500 continued to decline. Despite promises that the Federal Reserve's interest rate cuts would soon prop up the market, business spending continued to remain stagnant. And companies sought to either hoard cash or pay down their debts.

While in a bull market, the Wall of Worry represents sideline cash that might actually flow into stocks and drive the market up. Slope of Hope money represents cash being tossed into a market with bad fundamentals. But investors who do so aren't necessarily suckers. Certainly, short-term traders have much to fear from temporary rallies in a bear market that might inspire false hope. In July 2002, for example, the S&P 500 fell from 992 to 775. By August, it had rallied back to 966 but by October it had fallen to 776. Investors with short-time horizons might well have found their wealth obliterated during those months. More patient investors, however, might well look at the money not as having been destroyed but temporarily sidelined. Investors following a plan of dollar cost averaging, where money is put into the market no matter what its direction, were able to buy more shares more cheaply as the market fell. If they are able to hang on, they will experience more upside from the inevitable true recovery.

Of course, the Slope of Hope money is that sideline money that will eventually cause the end of the bear market and bring about the next bull run. The stock market is always a field of combat for investors with differing interests and points of view, and that's where the potential for making money lies.

You Can Time the Market

As an intellectual game and with reams of historical data, it's easy to see that the market goes up and down for both short and long periods of time. The natural inclination, on seeing this elementary news, is to declare that the key to successful investing is to never be in the market as it drops and to always be invested as it rises. No argument here. But try it and see what happens. Actually, don't. Save your money.

Market timing is also known by the moniker "momentum investing," and it means that you buy stocks that have had good runs over the past months, weeks, or (if you're a day trader) minutes and hope to ride the continuation of those trends. An investor could also buy into the whole stock market this way. One reason it's a popular approach is that it's easy. You don't have to worry about price or about a company's fair value, you just play the momentum that the market is offering.

One argument against momentum investing is that you will never know when an upward trend might end and turn south. The confident traders, of course, will argue that while they might indeed endure some losses as the trend starts its downward turn, they will find a way to sell the market before they have lost all the gains they made on the way up. But consider this argument: if you have to wait for trends to establish themselves before you invest, you might miss out on all the best gains. A $1000 investment in the market placed in 1925 would have been worth $2.6 million by the end of 2000—ups, downs, and sideways all turn into long gains over time. But those 900 months of investing are really dependent on 40 great months to generate that astounding return. Were you to have missed the 40 best months, that $1000 would have been worth just $15,000 after 75 years. Again, the great trader would argue that there's no way they'd have missed all 40 of those great months, but why risk missing any of them?

Buy-and-hold investing is just plain easier than market timing. Seventy-five years might seem like an inordinately long time horizon, and it is. But it is not completely out of line for a young investor today who might be building a 401(k) portfolio that will have to last as life expectancies rapidly grow toward 100 years and even beyond. Keep in mind what Wharton Professor Jeremy Siegel proved in his 1994 book, *Investing for the Long Haul*: Stocks have historically provided positive returns over 20 years.

There is a persuasive argument against the buy-and-hold model, articulated by Andrew Smithers and Stephen Wright in their book *Valuing Wall Street*. It says that choosing whether or not to be in the market is the most important part of investing and that buy-and-hold advocates, by definition, always think that it's a good time to be in the market. Smithers and Wright are correct here, as they are in most cases. (If it isn't obvious by now, *Valuing Wall Street* is definitely recommended reading for any investor.) But what they advocate as an alternative isn't market timing but a fundamental approach to deciding whether or not the stock market is overvalued.

Smithers and Wright rely on a metric called Tobin's Q ratio, developed by Nobel laureate James Tobin in 1969. The Q ratio compares the underlying assets of all the firms trading on Wall Street to the prices that they are being sold for. As earnings change more frequently than asset values, the Q ratio tends almost always to move based on fluctuations in stock prices. For investors who believe that buying stocks means buying company assets and that those assets should be purchased at the smallest possible premium to their actual value, the Q ratio is an indispensable tool.

Smithers and Wright argued, just before the crash of technology stocks, that the market was trading at too high of a multiple compared to the underlying assets and that it was due for a crash. They were right. Following their hypothesis, an investor should constantly track the Q ratio and should be out of the market when it's too high. That isn't momentum investing or market timing, it's a fundamental reaction to the price of stocks against the assets that companies own. It has nothing to do with "sentiment" or trying to figure out when the rest of the market will panic and when investors will become optimistic again.

Unfortunately, it's difficult for the average investor to get a clear picture of the assets held by corporate America (it took Smithers and Wright a lot of work), and most people's brokers won't be much help on this front. A technique that works but that is impossible to use won't help the average investor time the market.

Buy-and-hold believers argue that even the crash of 2000 is just a blip on the radar screen for the long-term investor. Eventually, they reason, the market will smooth out and stock returns of between 6 and 8 percent a year over the long haul will still be likely. Such returns don't seem like much, but they beat bonds and cash, and they add up over time.

It still seems that for most investors, buy and hold is the way to go. But keep the Smithers and Wright warning in mind: Sometimes the market is overvalued and due for a crash. If you can leave your money to ride for a long time, that might not matter. But if retirement is imminent or tuition bills are coming due, then at least some money should be kept in a safe, cash account so that important and immediate obligations aren't affected by a market downturn.

When Intel Sneezes, the Market Catches a Cold

Intel makes the myth, because it's a recent example. But there have been other companies that have been considered so fundamental to the American economy and to the stock market that they are thought to be market barometers. In 1952, president of General Motors Charles Erwin Wilson famously claimed that "what is good for the country is good for General Motors and what is good for General Motors is good for the country."

Big, sturdy chipmaker Intel earned its market-moving reputation during the 1990s because its chips and servers fueled the Internet boom. Though Intel is the subject of this maxim, the same could be said of Microsoft, which investors endowed with the cute name "Mister Softee" as a play on its ticker. Both of these stocks were popular during the 1990s because investors wanted to benefit from the Internet without giving up their principle of owning only profitable companies with proven business models. So they flocked to these stocks as if they were value plays. One other reason that Intel had such sway over the markets, and other technology stocks, is that the dotcoms and the major corporations who were fueling the dotcom boom, are both Intel customers. If Intel reports that chip sales are down, then computer sales are likely down across the board. If Intel says that server sales are down, then growth in Web-based businesses might be diminishing.

But it wasn't the technology bust that busted this myth. Intel actually missed earnings in the summer of 1999, and the Nasdaq reacted by gaining 39 points to finish at 2817, which was the twenty-fifth record finish for the Nasdaq in 1999. Perhaps, one could argue, the market should have reacted to Intel's sneeze since the Nasdaq collapsed a year later. But the point of the example is that there are sometimes other factors at work in the market that will overwhelm the results of any one company—even an important company like Intel. In the case of 1999, it was irrational exuberance.

Still, the performance of the largest stocks is important to any index investor. Most indexes are market-weighted, meaning that they represent more shares in the largest companies. Sure, the S&P 500 has 500 stocks, but the largest stocks in the bunch will dominate the performance of the index. In that case, a sneeze in any of the top five companies will surely have some effect on the index. If you go to a broader index, you will still see that the S&P 500's influence is the determining factor in returns. Since the S&P 500 represents stock with market caps of between $500 million and $300 billion, those stocks will dominate when they show up in another cap-weighted index like the all-inclusive Wilshire 5000. Though Vanguard offers both an [S&P] 500 Index Fund and a Total Market Stock Market Index Fund, founder John Bogle concedes that, historically, the performance for the total market and the S&P 500 are nearly identical.

That leaves an investor pondering the "Intel Sneezes" myth with a dilemma. Clearly, big stocks like Intel matter. Because they are likely to have business relationships with other companies in the market, they are a vital source of news and insight. Because they mean more to the indexes, they have a bigger effect on overall market performers than smaller stocks do. But big companies often have their own problems that do not reflect trends in the market at large.

If Intel sneezes because something is wrong with Intel, it shouldn't much matter to other stocks. If Intel sneezes because formerly high-flying companies have cut back on ordering product, then a clue is there. Only homework beyond watching the price number can tell you what the case happens to be.

There's also another factor to ponder: Since the end of the tech boom, Intel is out of favor, and people don't say this so much any more. Soon, the market will pick another stock that sneezes and transmits diseases. It will be an expression of yet another fad. It's important not to ignore the company that next wins that honor, but it's also important not to follow it blindly.

The Trend Is Your Friend

A fundamental assumption in this book says that stock pickers make money by being right when the rest of the market is wrong. The opposing view claims safety in numbers and is summed up by the old gambler's credo "when the train comes in, everybody rides." Following the trend is a market timer's technique. Its flaw is that trends don't last forever and there is no organized warning before the end. The myths of Wall Street are replete with contradictions. You will hear "the trend is your friend" quite a bit, maybe because it rhymes. Folks also used to say "don't fight the tape," although the phrase as fallen into disuse because, well, who has a stock tape running out onto the floor these days? But another saying, as much Wall Street wisdom as "the trend is your friend" is that "trend is not destiny."

To give "the trend is your friend" its due, let's first examine it in its strongest setting, in the world of day traders. For day traders, the trend really is a friend. Day trading involves sitting at a terminal watching ticker symbols and following their lines on charts. A stock will start going up and then it will start going down. Day traders will buy a stock as it climbs and wait for it to change direction. They let it drop a little (to be sure that a new trend is emerging) and then they sell it. This can happen in minutes, hours, or days. The idea is to take a few pennies on each trade, a nickel on a good one, but to be up by the end of the day. That kind of investing relies on nothing but trends. Day traders don't need to know anything about the companies they're putting money into—not even their names. It's all just tickers and fever charts for these investors.

Day trading is risky business. In a way, it's like playing a video game but it's even more difficult than that. If you have been moving a Playstation 2 character around a screen full of bloodthirsty enemies, you are still in a controlled environment. Hit the dragon with enough arrows and the dragon is programmed to die. There's predictability built into any video game. But stock market trends aren't preprogrammed and can start and change without a moment's notice. Selling when the stock starts to drop sounds easy, but what if there's no one buying? Making a few cents per share in a few minutes sounds easy, but can you make enough to cover your trading costs? Most folks aren't day traders and they shouldn't be.

Day trading is really just a civilian version of what Wall Street traders do every day. But there's a difference. A day trader plays with his own money. Wall Street traders use a firm's money. Their job is to respond to the needs of their firm, to buy and sell stocks on behalf of investors or the firm's trading accounts. They are trying to get the best possible deal on every trade, down to fractions of a cent, because when you are a firm trading millions of shares a day, those half pennies matter. For folks like this, a trend that lasts two hours can indeed be a friend—or a deadly nemesis.

If you're not a day trader, then this maxim holds less importance. If you're into using fundamental analysis as a way to pick stocks for a diversified portfolio, then these intraday trends don't matter a bit. Trend is not destiny. Some of the best value stocks are value stocks because they are downtrodden. The only way to choose a phoenix that will rise from the ashes is to buy in opposition to a trend because the bird has to be burnt before it can fly again.

There are, of course, longer trends that affect the retail investor. The Nasdaq has yet to rebound from its crash in the middle of March 2000. Pouring money into Internet stocks after the bubble burst would not have paid off. But that has nothing to do with trends. The bubble burst because it was fundamentally unsustainable. Too many companies that were losing money were trading at insane prices. An investor concerned with fundamentals, rather than trends, would have realized that fact and missed all of the technology gains—but also all of the subsequent losses. Even a favorable trend isn't the friend of a fundamental investor, because to the fundamentalist, trends don't matter.

This is easy to say, of course. In the moment, while the Nasdaq climbed toward 5000, nobody wanted to be left out. But that friendly trend gave no warning of its departure, did it? Trends, good or bad, are unreliable friends at best.

The Stock Market Rises as the Bond Market Falls

Stocks and bonds are asset classes in fundamental opposition to one another. Stock represents equity ownership in a company. Bonds represent a loan to a company or government. Stockholders are often borrowers, and bondholders are always lenders. Borrowers and lenders exist on opposite sides of a transaction, so it makes intuitive sense that the stock and bond markets would be similarly opposed.

For most investors, bonds, commonplace though they might be in the papers and on the news, are actually an esoteric topic. That's because very few investors own corporate bonds, and even portfolios of government bonds like Treasuries or local municipal bonds tend to be held through mutual funds. Though it's not uncommon for an investor to own stocks in a brokerage account, corporate bonds and even government bonds are generally owned through mutual funds, if at all.

To examine this myth, the bond universe has to be divided into its two major camps: corporate and government. Let's examine the logic behind this theory: Take a look at corporate bonds, for example. These tend to be held by institutions and to a lesser extent, wealthy individuals, and they represent the public debt of companies. Corporate bond investors want to know that the company is financially healthy and that it won't renege on promised interest payments or on the payment of principle to the bondholders. In that sense, corporate bondholders are aligned with ordinary shareholders because both depend on the long-term financial viability of the company. If the company is doing well, both its stock and bond prices should appreciate.

When it comes to Treasuries, representing the debt of the U.S. government, there is some reason to expect that the yields on these securities can affect the stock market. A bond's yield is its price divided by the interest rate that it pays. If the price is low, then the yield is high, because the interest rate, in most cases, doesn't change. Treasuries are a safe asset class, because the notion is virtually unthinkable that the U.S. government would become unable to make its interest or principal payments. That turn of events would certainly represent a financial crisis so severe that it would render all other problems and issues moot. Typically, investors use the stock market to generate higher returns, which they accept as compensation for the risk involved in stock investing. Treasuries, with no risk, generally offer piddling 1 percent to 3 percent returns. The stock market tends to offer 6 to 8 percent.

But what if the price of Treasuries dips to the point where the yield on the Treasury market is higher than the return offered by stocks? (This can happen during prolonged bear markets or during sideways markets.) Money might well flow out of stocks and into Treasuries, causing further price declines in stocks. Of course, all of that money moving into Treasuries would eventually raise Treasury prices, thus depressing the yield, making stock returns look appealing once more. That's the logic, anyway. The data is entirely inconclusive.

The idea that the stock and bond markets exist as foils to one another made a lot of sense for the first half of the twentieth century and that led to an enduring but unchecked myth. Take a look at the yield on 10-year Treasury bonds between 1998 and the beginning of 2003 and you will see that stocks and bonds moved in lockstep throughout the Internet boom. They didn't begin to diverge until well into the second quarter of 2003, and we have no idea whether or not that divergence will continue.

Says Lou Cranston, chief economist at Wrightson ICAP: "Stocks and bonds almost never moved with each other before 1960. After that, we began to develop markets where both stocks and bonds can rally together. In the 1980s, bonds served to drive stock prices and the two securities moved together. During the 1990s, stocks served to drive the bond market."

Knowing which asset class is driving the market is extremely difficult for the average investor, although bond gurus like PIMCO's Bill Gross can usually offer a clue in public comments.

Still, this matter might not be something that should overly concern the average investor. The stock market is best valued based on the fundamentals of stocks while the government bond market is valued based on how favorable it is to own U.S. debt in the face of inflation and other factors. Stocks are for investors who require substantial growth over a long period of time while bonds are for investors who require safety and are willing to give up return for it. It's best to judge each on its own merits.

Follow the Rule of 20

The Rule of 20 refers to what economists call an "inflation-adjusted price-to-earnings ratio." It basically says that in times of low inflation, the market exhibits higher P/E ratios. The notion is wonderfully intuitive: Low inflation means that the costs of living and doing business aren't rising quickly. In that environment, say Rule of 20 believers, investors are willing to pay a premium for corporate earnings that are unimpeded by a rise in costs for equipment and services or the diminished purchasing power of the dollar.

The notion makes some sense. Without inflation hindering profit growth at Intel, investors are better assured that the company will grow earnings in the future, and of course they will pay a premium for real earnings and the promise of more to come.

Here's where the "20" comes into play: If the P/E ratio of the stock market (basically the P/E of all the stocks, averaged) plus annualized inflation is under 20, then the market is fairly valued and will perform well in the future. If the inflation adjusted P/E is over 20, then the market has been overbought and is due for a nosedive.

Aside from passing the thought test, the Rule of 20 also passes the test of history, according to Glenn Tanner, an economics professor at Southwest Texas State University. In a 1999 paper for the *Journal of Financial and Strategic Decisions*, Tanner set up two scenarios over a 60-year time horizon. One thousand dollars invested in the market in 1935 and left to sit passively would be worth $134,000 by 1995. But if an investor put in $1000 in 1935 and then switched to Treasuries every time the adjusted P/E of the market topped 20 (and then went back into the market when the adjusted P/E fell), that person would cash out with $244,000 in the end.

Tanner also sought to prove that the Rule of 20 is better than the straight-up P/E ratio in terms of predicting market performance. The timing of Tanner's study might have had something to do with the debunking. When he began work on the paper, he sought to explain the positive investment returns enjoyed in 1995, when the stock market traded at a historically high 22 times earnings. By the time Tanner's paper was published in the fall of 1999, the market traded at 33 times earnings. Tanner's study ended during the glorious days of the long bull run. Inflation hasn't risen since the dotcoms crashed and burned, and, indeed, it is so low at the moment that some dire economists have begun whispering about the potential for deflation in the U.S. economy. The stock market, meanwhile now trades at less than 20 times earnings, which seems to suggest that the market did indeed revert to the proper Rule of 20 level.

That seems a vindication of the theory but remember that the Rule of 20 isn't the only way of thinking that foresaw a fall in equity prices. Andrew Smithers and Stephen Wright called it by saying that the market's Q ratio (measuring stock prices against corporate assets) was out of line. More traditional value players who believe that the proper price-to-earnings ratio for the market is between 12 and 15 (the S&P 500's historical average) also said that the market would fall, and they presumably believe it will fall yet further.

The problem is, in the summer of 2003, the market seems to be slowly edging toward a recovery. The Dow was above 9000 for the first time in a year, the Nasdaq offered an impressive 20 percent return, and the S&P 500 was up by 13 percent. According to the Rule of 20, there shouldn't be any room for upside in a market that hovered around the upper end of its reasonable low-inflation valuation after the 2000 sell-off. Already the S&P is trading at 30 times earnings, and only a fairly colossal crash would vindicate the rule.

It's possible that inflation, currently at less than 1.5 percent, is so low that 20 times earnings is now too low a multiple and the rule should become the rule of 23 or the rule of 25. We have no idea where this could lead.

It is true that inflation is generally bad for the companies represented by stocks, just as it's bad for consumers and private companies. But low inflation isn't always good for all companies. It might, for example, represent a lack of pricing power on behalf of the companies that sell goods and services. If companies can't get a good price for their products, profitability suffers and stocks will suffer along with it. The argument lately has been that increased productivity has brought down the cost of doing business and that companies haven't lost pricing power, they just don't need to charge so much to keep healthy margins.

It's clear then that anyone who wants to create an inflation-adjusted valuation for the stock market will have to explain why inflation is either high or low. It's also important for the stock selector to make sure that portfolio companies are actually benefiting from current economic circumstances.

As for the market, well, over the long term, it's grown, enduring a century of high and low inflation.

A Rising Tide Raises All Ships

At first glance, this maxim seems like a no-brainer, and it appears to be true. The market is, after all, an amalgam of stock prices. So for the market to be up, stock prices have to be on the rise, at least generally. When the market is up, an investor who picks stocks with darts should have an easier time than when the market is in decline. But even a bull market is full of losers, and the best of times for everyone can be the worst of times for the individual.

The way investors tend to measure the market obscures the fact that a strong market rally can be driven by a relatively small number of large stocks. The S&P 500 is a popular proxy but it's also what's known as a cap-weighted index. Companies with the largest market capitalizations make up the largest portions of the S&P 500. During the late 1990s, technology companies soared to higher market caps and thus, the rise in technology stocks made it look as if the entire market were on the rise. If you are an index investor, this situation doesn't present a problem. The market is going up and you are happy. But if you are a stock picker, it doesn't mean that you can choose stocks blindly and expect them to appreciate. Stocks do rise and fall in a bull market. On the news, financial reporters often talk about winners versus losers on a daily basis. The market can be up, even if the losers outnumber the winners, as long as the winners are up a lot.

During the late 1990s, the market rewarded companies that focused on technology, made a great show of using technology, or just sounded like they were somehow technological. Sure, investors in the total market did well as stocks climbed. The Vanguard Total Stock Market Index Fund climbed an average 25 percent a year between 1996 and the end of 1999. But there were losers, even during those happy days before reality set in on the markets.

But for stock pickers, placing your faith in a rising tide is a dangerous religious commitment. Remember that during the late 1990s there was a lot of talk about "value stocks" being "out of favor." Really, these stocks were out of flavor, and they were punished for their lack of trendy appeal.

Bethlehem Steel, an old company in a troubled industry, had an up-and-down year in 1999, while the markets were expanding rapidly. Bethlehem reached as high as $10 a share in April that year and dipped to below $6 in November while the S&P 500 rose 1.3 percent during that time period. Oil companies faced pressures during the late 1990s because a lot of economic expansion was helped along by low oil prices that cut into exploration and production profits.

It is true that bull markets tend to be populated by "bull market geniuses." They don't know much about the stock market but make a lot of short-term money by hitching a ride on the wave. This outcome is, of course, pure luck, and it is easier to get lucky when a mania that drives higher returns has taken hold. But even if you are a momentum investor who eschews any sort of fundamental stock analysis, you will want to be more careful than the "rising tides" mantra suggests you need to be.

One complaint from mutual fund managers during the late 1990s is that investors weren't satisfied with positive returns that trailed those offered by the inflating stock market. The investor has a reasonable complaint: Why should they pay for performance that can't match a cheap index fund? But the cause of the complaint is more interesting. These managers might have chosen stocks that were going up, but they weren't going up enough. Earning a positive return is only one part of investing. A good investor wants a reasonable return. If your stocks are appreciating by 1 percent a year, then they aren't worth the risk. A bank will do that for you.

This myth is, in the end, just an attempt to make investing easy during a bull market. The good news is that it is easier to invest while the market is going up and it's even easier to get lucky, but that doesn't mean it's actually easy.

A Random Walk on Wall Street

The stock market is so difficult to predict that investors might well believe that returns are random and that all of the news and analysis that surrounds the market is nothing but noise. Those cynics will find a few friends in academia who believe that the stock market is a "random walk." The argument is somewhat compelling, and the implications for the investor are enormous. If the hypothesis is completely true, for example, then there's no point in reading books like this or in worrying about investments at all.

Past performance is no guarantee of future returns. The random walk interpretation of Wall Street says that stock returns are unpredictable and unfathomable. The theory begins by accepting the premise of the efficient market hypothesis that says that at any given moment, stock prices represent all of the knowledge available to the trading community. If the market is efficient, then stock prices have to be random, because the market would know if prices were predictable. Traders would try to exploit that knowledge and in so doing, would eliminate their advantage. If the market is efficient, then future prices must be unknowable.

There's no doubt that future prices are hard to know. Consider all of the problems that professional stock analysts have when they try to place price targets on the stocks they cover: They're wrong all the time. In 1999, Jim Glassman predicted that the Dow would cross 30,000. Good thing he didn't say when. Maybe he'll even be right someday. (If he sticks to his prediction long enough, he's sure to be.)

Just because predicting stock prices is difficult doesn't mean it's impossible. Random walk adherents might someday find themselves trumped by a particularly clever application of chaos theory that will find a pattern in the randomness and reduce the stock market to—well, it would destroy the stock market, wouldn't it? The first people to figure out the formula would make money for a while, but soon everyone would be in on the act and all trading would cease as investors tried to one-up each other.

It seems as if random walk adherents should get out of the market entirely, as they can't count on the old buy-and-hold belief that while the market fluctuates in the short term it produces consistent, positive, long-term results in future years. According to this model, history means nothing and a long bull market that starts in 1982 could be met with either the largest bull run ever in 2004 or the worst and longest decline in history. One result would be no more likely than the other.

One argument against the random walk model is that the market has risen over time, whereas a random distribution would have so many ups and downs to it that the market would be flat in the long run. It would be the same result as the laws of chance dictate you would get with a coin toss: You are bound to get as many heads as tails, if you flip a coin long enough. Unfortunately, this argument violates what philosophers call the "Coperni-can principle." Copernicus taught us that the Earth is not the center of the universe. Philosophers have since borrowed this lesson to say that we should suspect any theory that assumes we occupy a special place in the cosmos or in history. Say we assume that the stock market has been around long enough so that the ups and downs would even themselves out to cre-ate a flat market. That would also assume that we are at some special place in history where we have allowed chance the time it needs to run its course and make its pattern clear. Perhaps we are in a random up cycle and all will be worked out over the next 50 or 100 years. There's no way to know.

The random walk model might be closer to the efficient market hypothesis that fathered it in that a "soft" interpretation seems to make the most sense. Perhaps the market is random in some instances and patterned in others. Figuring out specific moments, such as the price of stock of ABC Corporation at 2:30 P.M. three years from now, might well be impossible. But the general direction of the stock market, in the wake of a year of Fed-eral Reserve interest rate cuts, might be easier to figure out.

One good thing about the random walk model is that it reminds us of our ignorance. Most investors err on the side of confidence. Even if you don't believe that the market is a random walk, it's worth considering that there probably are aspects of the market that are impossible to predict. Other aspects may be so difficult to predict that the task just seems impossible.

The Market Is Efficient

The efficient market hypothesis says that, at any given time, securities prices represent all available information and that the market and every stock in the market are always fairly valued. While some individual investors might be buying or selling based on ignorance or mistaken assumptions, the market—the aggregate of all those individuals who are buying and selling—has got it right. If this is true, then it makes no sense to say that ABC Corporation is overvalued. The market has valued it perfectly. You would only know that ABC Corporation is due for a fall if you have access to some inside information, and then it would be illegal and unethical for you to trade ABC. Efficient market theorists believe that the stock market can never be beaten unless investors resort to illegal or unethical means.

Economist Eugene Fama developed the notion of the efficient market in a 1970 paper for *The Journal of Finance*. In his paper, Fama defined the concept of the efficient market as one where a collection of well-studied and intelligent investors compete with one another for profit and in the end create a market informed by the über-knowledge of all their trades. But he did not declare the stock market itself to actually be efficient; that has been the subject of intense debate in academia for more than 30 years. Your broker probably won't advocate this approach, because his job is to sell stocks to you and one of his tools for stock selling would be research from his firm's analysts. Those analysts, of course, would like to believe that they have access to information that the rest of the market doesn't.

The hypothesis is difficult to disprove because of the way it's written. Since stocks are priced by the sum of all available information, the market can, in fact, be wrong. But you'd never profit from that. Enron at its highs was fairly valued, according to the hypothesis, because news of fraud and deceit from within the company wasn't available to the investing public. When that information became available, Enron found a new, lower, but fair valuation. Fooling the market by withholding information doesn't invalidate the theory.

Of course, the theory has grown in popularity since the 1970s, as information has traveled more and more quickly through the Internet and as regulators have cracked down on the dissemination of inside information. Before the Securities and Exchange Commission enacted Regulation: Full Disclosure in 2000, a company might well give information about earnings or a management change to a favored analyst, thus creating an advantage for institutional and (sometimes) brokerage clients of that firm. Now that the SEC demands that corporate communication with one analyst, and even with the press, be shared with the public at large, such blips in the information pipelines have been eliminated. As technology and regulations improve, the efficient market hypothesis becomes more and more persuasive.

But the hypothesis isn't perfect, and experience proves it so. The legendary father of value investing, Benjamin Graham, warned in the 1930s that "the market price is frequently out of line with the true value; there is an inherent tendency for these disparities to correct themselves." We learned that lesson in the spring of 2000. An efficient market theorist might well argue that the Nasdaq was fairly valued at its high in March of 2000 and at half that level a few months later. But the fundamentals of the market really didn't change. Companies with growing revenues but earnings that existed only as future promises were the norm in 1999 and the norm at the end of 2000. Sentiment changed, but the information didn't.

Many technology and telecommunications executives were flummoxed by the market crash because they believed that the market demanded that they show sales growth by expanding at the expense of profits. In 1999, investors demanded that companies open operations in new territories or acquire rivals by using their stock as currency. In 2000, investors seemed to have changed their minds. Interpretation changed while the information was basically the same.

The history of the market is also replete with great stock pickers. Benjamin Graham is one. But there's also Peter Lynch, Warren Buffett, and Jeffrey Vinik. These are managers with long-term records of finding undervalued stocks. Have they been wrong? Of course. The market might be beatable but that doesn't mean it's easy. Buster Douglas once proved that Mike Tyson could be beaten. But I'd still never take a swing at the guy.

Perhaps there's a "soft efficiency" at work where the market often gets it right but is sometimes wrong. That seems to accurately describe the dangerous markets we face where there's just enough vulnerability to persuade an investor to try to win but very little chance of success.

Don't Invest on the Advice of a Poor Man

This seems like a self-evident piece of advice, because anyone with the secret to creating wealth would have used the secret for personal gain. This attitude doesn't have so much currency outside investing circles. Boxers have no problems hiring trainers that they could easily pound into the canvas and actors routinely take direction from people who can't carry themselves on stage. If "don't invest on the advice of a poor man" means that the best stock advice isn't available on Skid Row, it's probably true, though not necessarily. A business student working his way through graduate school poverty might well have a lot of useful advice about the stock market but no money to invest.

Warren Buffett famously quipped that Wall Street was one of the few places in the world where folks in limousines take advice from people who ride the subway to work. To a very rich man, a poor man might be someone pulling down six figures a year. To Warren Buffett, being an orthodontist doesn't count as being rich. On the other hand, a look at the Forbes 400 list of richest Americans shows that investment acumen and money don't necessarily go hand in hand. Every year, for example, there's a list of "drop-offs," many of whom are entrepreneurs who held on to large swaths of company stock as it declined. Martha Stewart, for example was on the list in 2001 and off it in 2002 after a 60 percent decline in the shares of Martha Stewart Living Omnimedia. Wealth is not omniscience.

Meanwhile, there are plenty of great investors who aren't members of the Forbes 400. Take Peter Lynch, for example. One of the greatest stock pickers of all time, Lynch isn't on the Forbes 400. Sure, he's no doubt well off, if only because of his performance bonuses during the 1980s. Would you say that Bill Gates, worth $63 billion, is a better investor than Lynch, or is he a better entrepreneur?

Stock analysts often know quite a bit about the market. While they are often well paid, they don't rise to astronomical standards of wealth. They routinely sell stocks to and advise chief executives who are far wealthier. The whole scandal around the "spinning" of IPO shares, where analysts helped executives get in on new stock issues in exchange for investment banking business, would never have happened had the executives been unwilling to take advice from people who had less money than they did. That might be a strange way of making the point, so here's a more prosaic example: The JPMorgan Private Bank caters to wealthy clients who usually have accounts worth $25 million. The managers of those accounts don't generally have that much money to invest but they're still trusted by their clients.

The rich are often happy to leave their investments in the hands of poorer folk because they have better things to do with their time than to sit around watching the stock market. So it's at least true that the rich don't mind taking advice from the relatively poor.

It is of course, important to know the track record of whomever you have picked as your adviser. Returns over a long period (10 years, if possible) should be examined for mutual fund managers. The National Association of Securities Dealers will offer information about stockbrokers so that botched stock picks that resulted in arbitration claims or lawsuits can be brought to light.

The important things to consider when choosing an investment adviser or manager are track record, acumen, and honesty. Net worth has little to do with it.

The Perfect Portfolio Never Needs a Trade

The perfect portfolio is the portfolio an investor never has to worry about. The stock choices will all steadily and reasonably gain value over time and will perhaps even pay out dividends along the way. But the perfect portfolio doesn't exist. Warren Buffett has famously remarked that his preferred holding period for a stock is "forever." But that's well known for being impractical advice. Why are you investing? Clearly, to make money. Why money? Clearly, to spend money. A stock that's never sold is money that's never spent, and in the end, no matter how you look at money, the eventual spending is the reward.

It might be better stated that the perfect portfolio never needs a desperate trade because it's made up of solid companies with transparent finances and that life keeps it free of surprises.

The perfect portfolio should also be free of excessive trading. Trading costs money. Even most online brokerages will charge $15 per transaction. That's 3 percent on a $500 trade and 1.5 percent of $1000 transaction. The first hurdle a portfolio has to overcome is to make back the costs associated with setting up the portfolio in the first place. The market, on average, returns between 6 and 8 percent a year. If transaction costs add up to 3 percent that means that half of the market's gains do nothing for the investor but pay for the initial trade. Slow and careful trading reduces brokerage fees and increases profits.

Trading is also punished by the government, which taxes all capital gains. Long-term capital gains are incurred when an investor sells a security after holding it for 18 months, and they are currently capped at 15 percent of profits. Short-term gains are taxed at an investor's income level, which can be as high as 35 percent. The taxman clearly rewards patience.

Since few of us are as skillful as Warren Buffett, the perfect portfolio where every stock appreciates reasonably over a long period of time will be impossible to attain, so make the best of what you have. The good news is that the tax consequences to realizing a loss are always positive.

The perfect portfolio is, like Utopia, an imaginary construct. If it imparts the lesson that an itchy finger over a mouse that's aimed at the Web site of an online brokerage is a bad thing, then this is a useful myth. Reality of course, sometimes demands a trade or two, though. So respond to reality, but act with the ideal in mind.

A Paper Loss Is Not a Loss

Every transaction has two sides. First a stock is purchased and later a stock is sold. A loss or gain isn't considered "realized" until both sides of the transaction are complete. Given enough time, an investment that loses money on paper might turn around and become profitable. The possibility leads a lot of investors to hang on to losers and then, when they need cash, they sell their winners. It's a disastrous strategy. Certainly, all investments need enough time to play out, and there's no sense in always selling at the first sign of loss. But, sadly, a loss is a loss, even when it's unrealized.

While it's important to hold stocks through their dips, if you believe in their prospects, it's also important, when judging overall portfolio performance, to be honest about what's up and what's down. For one thing, losses aren't necessarily a bad thing because losses can be used to offset taxes on gains.

Don't get too crazy about not paying taxes. In the end, we all want to pay taxes because paying taxes is what happens when you make money. But at the end of every year it is important to take a look at your winners and losers and to figure out what losers are worth dropping overboard.

Looking for losses is also a good way of finding time to think about your stock selections. Your losing money doesn't make you a bonehead, and it doesn't mean you're wrong. If you think the market is wrong about a stock in your portfolio, it might be a good time to buy some more stock while it is cheap.

Unfortunately, there's no magic formula that says whether you should sell a stock. Some investors, when it comes to weeding out losers, set a personal stop-loss. They say that they can afford to lose no more than 5 percent on any investment. Once a stock dips below 5 percent and stays there for a reasonable period of time, they sell.

Whether or not you need a stop-loss depends on your personality. If you are insanely stubborn and willing to lose the farm to make a point, a stop-loss frees you from emotional involvement. All decisions are made "by the numbers." The stock failed, you didn't.

At the same time, not every investor needs a stop-loss. If you are confident in your analysis, it's perfectly reasonable to hold on to a falling stock and to wait for a rebound. It's important to know that you're making a rational decision and that it might be wrong, and it's important to reexamine the stock's fundamentals and to ask, "Would I buy this stock today?" But it's also all right to buck the trend every now and then. Being right while the market is wrong is how some of the best managers make money. Just remember that it's hard to do, and make sure that at some point you can let go and call it quits.

One thing to keep in mind, after all: A sold stock can always be bought back later.

The P/E Ratio Works for Stocks but Not for the Market

You will often see economists talking about the price-to-earnings ratio of the stock market, as it's one of the most popular methods for figuring out whether the market is overvalued or fairly valued. The P/E ratio is also used as a way of valuing stocks, especially by investors who believe that what they are really buying when they buy a stock is a piece of the company's earnings. One thing to keep in mind is that, by itself, the P/E ratio means little. The P/E ratio works best as a tool for valuation, when it can be compared to another P/E ratio. With stocks, that's easy because there are plenty of stocks. For the market, it's impossible because there's only one.

If I say that Microsoft is trading at 20 times earnings, I haven't told you anything about whether or not Microsoft is a good deal. If I say it's trading at 20 times earnings while all of the other companies in the software sector are trading at 25 times earnings, and if I then explain that Microsoft will surely catch up to the sector, then I've told you something.

Similarly, the P/E multiple of the S&P 500 (the prices of all the stocks over the earnings of all the stocks) can be used for comparative purposes. If I'm trying to sell you a value-oriented mutual fund, I might say, "The fund's holdings trade at 17 times earnings while the stocks in the S&P 500 trade at 29 times earnings." You will at least then know that the value manager is being true to her word and picking the cheaper stocks on the market.

What you'd like to do, of course, is to use the P/E ratio of the S&P 500 to figure out if the market is fairly valued or not, and that's just never going to work. For one thing, there's nothing to compare it to except history. During the late 1990s, the P/E ratio of the S&P 500 topped 35 and analysts warned of a crash because those stocks historically trade at 15 times earnings. Well, the market eventually did crash. (If you keep saying the market will crash, you will be right sooner or later.) But the P/E ratio of the S&P 500 never dropped back down to 15. If there were some market juju at work to pull the P/E ratio back to the mean, it should have happened. But it didn't.

Andrew Smithers and Stephen Wright, in their emerging classic book, *Valuing Wall Street*, pick apart the use of the P/E ratio to value the market. They warn that in the past, it has given "a disastrously wrong indication of value." In the early 1930s, they say, earnings were so depressed that the P/E ratio for the market was sky-high, despite low stock prices. But between 1930 and 1935, the market actually rallied. The period was simply such a terrible time for earnings that the P/E ratio didn't give an accurate picture of the market.

Since the market never did return to a P/E multiple of 15, it's possible that investors have become comfortable with higher valuations for the broad market. That reveals a bit of why P/E ratios work for stocks but not the market as a whole. Comparing software companies based on their earnings multiple is a fair, apples-to-apples comparison. Comparing current events to historical norms is trickier and perhaps a better job for market historians than today's stock pickers.

No Tree Grows to Heaven

If it's hard to admit a mistake and to sell off bad picks for a loss, it's even harder to sell a stock that's been a boon to the portfolio. Like a gambler on a roll, it's tempting to want to hang on to a good stock just a little bit longer. Many investors fear missing opportunity more than they fear incurring losses. Of course, stocks go up and they go down. The key to making effective use of the saying is to remain a long-term investor while still realizing the need to sell winners every now and then.

First, it is true that some trees get pretty close to heaven. That's a good argument for hanging on to stocks when it seems reasonable to do so. Microsoft is trading at 359 times its 1986 IPO price (a split-adjusted 7 cents) right now. It's way too late to get in on the Microsoft public offering, of course, but that is a pretty heavenly figure. The stock has gone up and down in its 17 years as a public company, but on the whole it's up and has rewarded its long-term shareholders.

Microsoft is a famous exception, of course. Amazon.com shot up past $400 a share, and it never should have. There's a winner that should have been sold before the stock collapsed to the low teens. The stock has recently recovered to a respectable $32 a share, but it seems safe to predict that the high-flying days are over. The best stock picks will invariably become too expensive to own. That's the point, really; it's victory for the investor.

The price-to-earnings multiple is the best way to tell if a stock has appreciated too quickly, because you are, in the end, buying the company for those earnings. Use trailing earnings, because you want to be sure that the money has actually been booked and isn't promised.

Ideally, the multiple shouldn't change much. If earnings for a company grow at 10 percent a year, the stock price shouldn't inflate too much more than 10 percent. Obviously, since the price per share will be greater than the earnings per share at the outset, a 10 percent increase in both will create some expansion in the P/E ratio. But at least you know that the rise in price is in line with the rise in earnings. The P/E multiple could also be checked against industry peers. Suppose it's much higher than the rest and there is no good reason for it (for example, if the company doesn't have dominant market share in the sector). Then the stock has probably risen too quickly, and a decision to hang on is a bit like taking another spin at the roulette wheel.

For stocks without past earnings, estimated earnings aren't a reasonable substitute, because earnings estimates become less accurate the farther out the forecast. Keep in mind that a lot of unprofitable companies don't survive until that magic quarter where they promise profitability. Also remember that companies often go to great lengths to become profitable for a quarter but then can't sustain it. Try monitoring the price-to-trailing-sales ratio, and demand to see margin improvement if that ratio starts growing beyond the rate of sales growth over a year. These ratios can also be easily compared to industry peers. As with the P/E ratio, if the company is trading at a price that makes it more expensive than the companies around it, there had better be a compelling reason for it.

The big gainers in a portfolio demand this kind of special attention because it is tempting to hold on for too long. Remember, of course, that the price you paid is an important consideration as well. If you took a risk on a hot stock that was already a bit overpriced when you bought it, then a quarterly or even monthly evaluation of the holding is a necessary ritual. Stocks purchased more cheaply that are meant to be a core component of the portfolio shouldn't necessarily be traded just because they are going to fall off their highs a bit. A good long-term return is sought so a few missed opportunities to sell are just something that has to be endured. Stocks can fall off their highs without collapsing.

The point is not to hang on to high-flying stocks that will plummet past the purchase price. Momentum investors who buy stocks on their way up no matter what they are paying for earnings have to be particularly wary and vigilant about using their guys to tell them when heaven is a bit too close for comfort. I wish them luck.

For the fundamental investor, this is just yet another reminder for them to take a look at their portfolio every now and then to make sure success hasn't blown a stock beyond its proper proportions.

Never Check Stock Prices on Friday;
It Could Spoil the Weekend

A stock portfolio is part of life—but not the most important part. So investors feel a need to be able to put it to the side every now and then. Keeping stock discussions out of weekend life is one technique that's commonly employed. But since most investors aren't professional investors, this advice might not be the most practical one. A lot of families do their financial business over the weekend out of necessity, and that endeavor might mean checking the returns at the end of the week. We will deal with the issue of Friday returns in the maxim "Buy on Monday, Sell on Friday," because this myth really has more to do with an investor's psyche than it does the market.

In a way, there's a good argument to be made for valuing your portfolio only on Fridays. Since there's no trading on Saturday or Sunday, you will have to actually think things through before making a decision to buy or sell stock based on the week's numbers.

Weekends are also a calm time for the markets in terms of news because the major newspapers, Web sites, and financial networks will be spending their time analyzing what happened in the week that just ended and looking forward to the week that's about to begin. During the week, news services are concentrating on breaking stories, and these days, with so many outlets producing breaking news and even breaking commentary, the investor is often left inundated and confused. The weekend provides a good time to think everything through. That's more important now than ever because, though the 24-hour cable stations have certainly had their shining moments when it comes to breaking big stories, they have also been known to over-hype a tale or two in order to have something to put on the air. One recent example would be the outbreak of severe acute respiratory syndrome (SARS) in late March of 2003. An investor reacting to initial coverage of the disease might well have thought that the 1918 Spanish Flu epidemic was about to happen all over again. It took months for the true story to unfold, which is that SARS is a nasty cousin of the common cold and that, although it must be vigilantly dealt with, it won't destroy the global economy.

The United States is quickly evolving into a 24-hour-a-day society, with only a few institutions like government agencies and financial services holding on to a 9-to-5 schedule and a five-day workweek. Even banks have used technology to make savings account withdrawals possible at 2:00 A.M. on a Sunday just about anywhere in the world. In most cases, this development represents progress. But it's fortunate that Wall Street hasn't jumped on board, and that's an important exception. I might suggest that investors check stock prices only on Fridays because there's a built-in cooling-off period before the market opens again.

The myth of stock investing is that it's supposed to be as frenetic as Wall Street. It isn't. If you want to talk in hand signals, bark into telephones, and spend your lunch hour making executive trades with one hand while holding a sloppy deli sandwich in another, then get a job with a major Wall Street firm. Those guys are playing with other people's money. When it comes to your money, be calm, take your time, and let the suited monkeys in the financial district jump around on your behalf.

Enjoy your weekend.

Never Buy on Margin

Most conservative investors will eschew the idea of buying stocks on a margin loan because it can involve risking more money than the investor actually has available. Your broker, wanting to pad her company's account with some interest charged to you, will at some point want to lend you money for investment purposes. Whether or not you take the loan is up to you.

One thing that's great about margin is that it isn't your money, but it can be used to make money. It is also a loan given on usually favorable terms. Your portfolio is the collateral for the loan, so the bank is fairly well assured that it's going to get its money back. There's a limit to how much margin money you can have, set by the Federal Reserve, although every lending bank's rules differ, sometimes from client to client. Typically, you can have about 20 percent of your portfolio's value in debt.

In good times, that stipulation doesn't matter much, but you have to realize that offering up your portfolio as collateral gives the lender a great deal of control. If the value of securities you have bought falls and the loan stands at more than 20 percent of your portfolio, you will get what's called a margin call. It means you either have to pump cash into your account to keep the loan below its 20 percent ceiling or have to sell stocks that you might prefer to hang on to in order to pay off, or pay down, the loan. Depending on an investor's standing with the brokerage house, the margin limits might be higher or lower than 20 percent. The Federal Reserve requires that half of a leveraged stock's market value be kept in the custody of the brokerage house as collateral for the margin loan. Although the Fed hasn't changed that requirement in years, setting the margin collateral limit is one of the central bank's jobs. It's always possible that the Fed would raise those limits, if it thinks that too many investors are borrowing money to participate in a speculative bubble. That notion was frequently discussed during the last stock boom.

Margin money shouldn't be used for the purchase of anything but liquid securities, just like general-purpose loans shouldn't be used to purchase stock. Don't laugh. A fair number of goofballs took credit card advances to buy stocks during the late 1990s. It worked for a while, when the market was dwarfing the 14 percent interest fees charged by the credit cards. Then it stopped working. Similarly, during the bubble, people who owned high-flying stocks found themselves rewarded with more access to margin money, and they used it for things like cars and homes. Since those items are difficult to sell, it's impossible to make a margin call.

The one safe thing about using margin to purchase stocks is that if you are on the ball and sell your stock during a disaster, you can keep the losses confined to your portfolio and not wind up the permanent debtee of a bank. It might wipe out your entire portfolio, but it won't wipe out your entire financial life.

It's best, for reasons of control, to keep margin away from money you will need immediately. Such money probably shouldn't be in the stock market anyway, but it certainly shouldn't be used to make leveraged purchases.

Mutual Funds Are Safer Than Individual Stocks

The best mutual funds offer smart management and instant diversification at a reasonable price. It's just common sense that a well-managed, diversified portfolio is going to be safer than any one stock out there or than a portfolio of stocks that's been cobbled together with less-than-skillful precision.

The problem is that there are 5000 mutual funds out there, and new ones are starting up every day. So mutual fund picking is becoming as difficult as stock picking. It's actually even more difficult, because mutual funds don't tend to earn a lot of attention from analysts and the media. They seem more content to follow individual stocks and companies. Mutual funds are by no means risk-free, and in some cases they are riskier than stocks.

Consider a rather tame mutual fund like an S&P 500 index. According to the RiskMetrics Group, a spin-off from JPMorgan that provides risk-return analyses to retail and institutional clients, the stock of Procter & Gamble actually carries less risk than the entire S&P 500. That means, basically, that Procter & Gamble's stock is less subject to price volatility than the index or any of the myriad of mutual funds out there that are more volatile than the S&P 500. But that doesn't mean that investors should pull all of their money out of the stock market and plow it into Procter & Gamble (and the Risk-Metrics Group knows this, of course), because there's no sense in banking entirely on the fortunes of one home-products corporation. Besides, Procter & Gamble is an exception.

The other side of the story is that a lot of stocks are riskier than the S&P 500, and you don't have to leave the arena of well-known companies to find them. IBM, Amazon.com, Microsoft, Ford, and Yahoo!, to name a few, are all riskier than the S&P 500, and they are riskier than a lot of managed mutual funds as well.

In the wide world of managed and index-following mutual funds, there are plenty of great products and plenty of bombs. The once-loved and now often-jeered Janus Fund, which returned an impressive 47.1 percent in 1999, is down 1.7 percent for the last five years after enduring big losses in

2000, 2001, and 2002. Over three years, the fund trailed the S&P 500 by 9 points. Just like stocks, mutual funds lose money.

Aside from performance risk, mutual funds also carry tax risks that you won't find in a self-made portfolio of stocks. To the government, a mutual fund is an investment company. It buys and sells stocks for a profit, and it pays taxes on those profits, usually in the form of either long-term or short-term capital gains. If you buy stock in ABC Corporation for $20 and sell it for $30, you'll pay taxes on $10. The $20 sum is called your cost basis. The same holds true for a mutual fund, but there's a difference as far as you're concerned.

Say that the fund buys ABC Corporation at $20. By the time you invest in the fund, ABC is at $33. But things turn sour and ABC drops to $25. The fund manager decides to sell. The fund is now liable for taxes on $5 and that tax burden is distributed to investors like you, even though you were only around to watch the price fall and reaped none of the benefits from the stock rising. Real life is even more complicated than that example because funds buy and sell so many stocks. A fund can be down for a year but still up over the course of its life, meaning that it can generate taxes even as the market falls. There's always a chance, especially when managers have to sell stocks to meet redemptions, that you could lose principal because of the fund's performance and be charged capital gains taxes by the government. That will never happen with your individual stock portfolio, where you control your cost basis and can sell losers in order to offset gains. This tax risk is unique to mutual fund investing. During the 2000 bear market, mutual fund investors were hit with $345 billion worth of capital gains charges even though the market lost $240 billion.

Also, mutual funds carry fees, and these create another risk, of sorts. The worst of the lot are the mutual funds that are sold by stockbrokers and financial advisers. These often carry a 5.75 percent sales charge (also known as a front-end load) that is split between the broker and the fund management company. Mutual fund companies love this because it means that they can get brokers to hawk their wares in exchange for a commission, and thus they don't have to bear the full costs of marketing their own products. Paying the load might not seem so bad, but remember, it means that the investment starts down nearly 6 percent on the very first day. Avoid starting in the hole by purchasing no-load mutual funds with low expense ratios.

Also, be aware that some funds have put redemption fees in place. (They have done so in an effort to stop day traders from jumping in and out of the fund in an attempt to make a buck on daily market fluctuations.)

Those fees will cost you money, if you need to withdraw in a given time period. You can sell a stock any time you want, but that option is not available for all mutual funds.

Finally, watch out for the management fee. The average fee that a manager will charge for a U.S. domestic equity index fund is 1.4 percent. There are better bargains available, if you look, so don't pay more than you need to. These fees can eat into returns over long periods of time. So, the less you pay, the more you will keep.

The Markets Abhor Uncertainty

The market is a great collection of people and not a machine that gives wholly logical assessments of the economy or the performance of the companies that are traded as securities. Everything in the outside world from teeny-bopper trends to geopolitical minutiae eventually finds expression in the great psychological maelstrom of the market. Television commentators are especially fond of saying that the markets abhor uncertainty, which is a way of explaining downward and sideways movements after natural disasters or before wars are fought. So the market abhors uncertainty, just as we all do.

But that doesn't adequately explain why markets behave by dropping or going stagnant during uncertain times. Let's take the example of early 2003 to see what psychological factors were at work on Wall Street.

First, with unemployment up to a historically blah but recently very high 5.8 percent, many retail investors were hoarding cash out of fear that they could lose their jobs and need their savings in order to pay rent.

Companies, though reporting higher earnings than dismal 2002, had used cost cutting to get there, and projections for growth were still muted. And plans of expansion were merely whispered, if stated at all.

Before the startlingly brief war with Iraq, pundits and economists wondered whether or not we were about to engage in a prolonged military action that could further balloon the U.S. budget deficit. They also speculated that the war might provoke terrorist attacks on U.S. soil. They may still be right, and the ramifications of current events might not be felt for years. But the immediate economic reaction to a busy and uncertain news year has so far been a recovery, with the S&P 500 jumping 14 percent and proving its first substantial positive returns since 1999.

The problem with trying to pinpoint and take advantage of uncertainty is that it's, well, uncertain. The collective intelligence behind the market might well react positively to situations that seem negative. But the reverse has also been known to happen.

Though this book advocates taking a thoughtful and analytic approach to stocks, the market, and investing in general, it is possible to overthink the news. That warning has become a bit of a truism, and it doesn't say much about when thought becomes overthought. Usually, the mistake occurs when we try to predict the culture's reactions to current events. The market and the minds that make the market tend to be unpredictable. In May of 2003, for example, on the exact day that the unemployment rate jumped from 6 percent to 6.1 percent, the Dow Jones Industrial Average grew to over 9000 for the first time in nearly a year. The reason, so the pundits say, is that the market had expected unemployment to go to an even higher level than it did; thus, bad news turned into good news over a single day of trading. That kind of collective, counterintuitive thinking is difficult to predict.

The financial structure of society is also more able to deal with uncertainty today than it has been at any other time. In part that's because of enhanced communication and information sharing, and in part because of enhanced regulatory requirements for major financial institutions. In April of 2003, when the SARS story was really picking up steam, there was a "run" on a bank in New York's Chinatown. Now, a bank run used to be an especially scary event: Depositors clenched their statements in their fists and screamed for their money. If the bank didn't have enough cash in its vaults, a riot could occur and the bank might fail. The Chinatown bank run caused nothing but long lines and headaches for tellers. The bank had the money, and if it didn't, it could have quickly gotten more through an interbank loan. Had the bank failed, the government would have made whole every depositor with less than $100,000 in his or her account. So uncertainty over something like a disease outbreak can't crash a bank these days. And news of a bank run, once a cause for major concern all through the financial markets, can now be dismissed as an almost anachronistic oddity.

It's true, of course, that events like the terrorist attacks on New York City and Washington, D.C., on September 11, 2001, can cause severe financial shocks that are felt by the stock market. But the U.S. economy is such a behemoth that the effect of such events will almost surely be temporary. Since events are not predictable, it's best to ride out the shocks of uncertainty. Perhaps, with diligence and care, you can find buying opportunities while the market panics.

Invest Money When You Have It

Most of us aren't blessed with gobs of money. We get paid every two weeks, meet our living expenses, and try to squirrel some money away. Outside of your taking advantage of your company's 401(k) plan, entering the market can be difficult. Sure, anyone can play, but it isn't free. Because of that, there's a temptation to stay on the sidelines until a big sum of money comes along that can be invested. The problem is, that money never seems to come along.

It makes sense to invest money as it comes in. Getting started is the hardest part, while adding to an existing portfolio can become a habit. But be smart about it. If you have only $1000 to invest, then don't open an account with a discount broker unless you get free trades right off the bat. If you pay $15 for your first trade, then that's like paying a 1.5 percent management fee on your $1000. You're better off buying an index fund from Vanguard that will charge 0.18 percent and give you exposure to the entire market rather than just one stock. Remember that, when you're paying per trade, the more money you have, the less you're paying in terms of a percentage. The percentage is in a sense more important than the dollar amount of the fees. That's because the percentage will tell you what kind of performance the investment will have to earn in order for you to win back the fee money.

Unfortunately, the market is fraught with barriers to entry. Most mutual funds demand that you make a minimum investment that's usually about $1000. And most brokerage houses want you to have at least $5000 before you open an account. For a middle-class family living paycheck to paycheck, it might take months or even more than a year to come up with enough cash to make a minimum investment. Though these four-figure sums are treated as chump change in the financial press and on television, they can seem daunting to an investor just starting out. But they shouldn't be a stopping point. One easy way into the market is through a corporate 401(k) plan, because there are no minimums. If you have access to a 401(k) plan at work, take advantage of it.

Otherwise, save and get into the market in the most diversified way possible. (Shares of a low-cost S&P 500 index fund are a great way to start.) Once you have met the initial hurdle, there's no reason to save up money to make additional investments. The technique of dollar cost averaging allows you to add a fixed sum of money into the market on a fixed schedule. Again, be careful. Some funds and brokerage houses will only let you increase the size of your accounts by a fixed sum, say $500. But most will let you add any amount once you have met the initial investment criteria.

Dollar cost averaging also has advantages over lump-sum investing. Dollar cost averaging is a bulky term that means investing a set amount of money ($500, $5000, $10,000) in the stock market at predetermined intervals (weekly, monthly, quarterly, annually), no matter what the market is doing. Some brokers will let you set up this kind of program well in advance so that when those dates roll around money will be transferred from a savings account into the market. Any investors with a 401(k) program are dollar cost averaging, whether they know it or not. The paycheck arrives once every two weeks and a certain percentage is shuffled off into the market.

The technique is appealing in its ease. Investors don't have to follow the market and try to pick the right time to jump in. Instead, the method kind of assumes that any time is a good time to get into the market.

In a way, that blithe assumption is correct. Put money into a rising market and it goes right to work. Put money into a falling market and you get more shares that can appreciate during a recovery. Tossing money into a falling market can be disheartening for investors who like to look at their statements all of the time. But remember that the cash isn't evaporating; it's being converted into shares. The worst mistake the dollar cost averaging investor can make is to lose sight of that fact and to opt not to make contributions in a falling market. Buying only when the market is on the rise increases the odds of buying at the moment when things are best and are about to crash. It's a nearly sure path toward buying high and selling low.

If the money is going into an account made up of individual stocks, dollar cost averaging is potentially a more expensive way of investing. That $15 brokerage fee is 15 percent of a $100 investment but only 3 percent of a $500 investment. Make a $100 investment five times and the total fee is $75, while the lump-sum investor has paid only $15 to invest the same amount. The other problem with the all-stock account is that most accounts won't allow for fractional share ownership.

Mutual funds don't have this problem. In fact, 401(k) investors own lots of fractional mutual fund shares. Some brokerage accounts that follow the "folio" model, in which stocks are arranged as a basket of securities, allow for fractional share ownership. A good example of this can be found at Foliofn.com.

The greatest advantage to dollar cost averaging is that it's a discipline that's easy to stick to. Once investors have decided to follow this path, they are free from the anxiety of trying to enter the market at just the right moment.

If a Trend Cannot Continue, It Will Not Continue

This one sounds like it came from a stock broker fan of Yogi Berra. But it actually has its roots with economist Herb Stein, who created what's known in economics as Stein's law: "Anything that can't go on, won't." What this doesn't say is when the end of a trend will show up. Without that crucial piece of information, this isn't useful as a market-timing device.

During the recent resurgence in gold prices, for example, a lot of money managers who have been derisively known as "gold bugs" claimed victory after 20 years of championing a metal that had been a terrible investment. It's great to see people happy, of course, but to stick with one idea for 20 years and then to crow when it finally comes about is ridiculous. Every sector of the stock market, every commodity, every type of bond, from Treasuries to junk, has had its day and will have its day again. Sometimes, those days are a very long way off. But single-minded devotion offers everyone the chance to be right, with even less frequency than a stopped clock.

People who call the ends of trends often suffer from the same uselessness. There are unrelenting bears who invest in and comment on the stock market. They're always waiting for a crash, and they always get one, because every now and then the market crashes.

As soon as it does, the irrepressible bulls start predicting a recovery. In 2001 and 2002, pundits predicted a "better second half of the year" every year. Then they repeated the predictions in 2003, and it seems like they are right. Fortunately for them, they didn't have to wait as long as the gold bugs.

Trends, both at the start and finish, are basically impossible to call. But the business of calling trends employs a lot of people, so they try. In the end, though, Stein's law, as channeled through Yogi Berra, seems like the only one that makes sense. All trends end—when they're over.

How the Market Reacts to News
Is More Important Than the News

Once investors cozy up to the belief that the market represents collective knowledge and sentiment, it's hard not to accept that whatever the market chooses to believe is, at least temporarily, as good as fact. If every investor in the world decides that the sun sets in the east and they invest that way, is there any point to investing otherwise based on superior data?

Stock market watchers speak more frequently about sentiment than they do about knowledge. Sentiment is a telling word here because what the market really expresses through all those prices set on a daily basis is a feeling about current circumstances and the impact of those circumstances on the future. The stock market is a great repository of news, rumor, and information. All of it is shared, gawked over, and, finally, interpreted and expressed as sentiment. So this collective sentiment rises from the interpretation of information offered by the market's various participants. They are all trying to use information to make money, of course, so their goal is to be as accurate and rational as possible. The interpretation should be right, after all, and it should create a lasting market sentiment in favor of a given investment decision.

Of course, says Aristotle, majority opinion doesn't make something true. In other words, 50,000 Frenchmen can be wrong. That's great news for stock pickers, who count on the market being wrong from time to time. In daily trading, a lot of news gets hyped beyond its proportion. Richard Freeman, the manager of the Smith Barney Aggressive Growth Fund, has held onto stock in Tyco through all sorts of scandals. He does so because he believes that it's a strong business and that whatever punishment Wall Street metes out on bad news will be temporary. Morningstar has rated his fund in the top 1 percent of performers in its category for more than a decade. In 2003, after the worst of Tyco's scandals that saw its chief executive step down and a shakeup of the company's board, the company's stock is up 5 percent. And that's in the face of a $6 billion lawsuit from investors trying to recoup losses from the company's earlier indiscretions. If, as the months progress, it looks as if the investors will win their lawsuit, Tyco's stock will almost certainly take another hit. But you can bet that, whatever Richard Freeman does with his fund's Tyco position, the lawsuit and the market's reaction to it won't be the driving force behind his decision.

In the long run, most market reactions to major news events, be they political, economic, or company-specific, are forgotten, because all that matters is that traders are trying to make money in real time. Last year's scandal is quickly forgotten as this year's earnings meet expectations.

A lot of market reaction is nothing more than noise that tends to fade. The long-term investor can't trust it and should be too busy reading financial statements to pay attention anyway.

Don't Overdiversify

An investor who is trying to beat the market has to own fewer stocks than are on the market. Owning more is impossible. Owning everything creates a portfolio that's identical to the market. So the only option available is to own less.

You might own too many stocks. A study by Standard & Poor's shows that concentrated mutual funds—funds with at least 30 percent of their assets in their top 10 holdings—have outperformed their more diversified peers by 1 percentage point (annualized) for the 10 years ended March 31, 2003.

One such concentrated fund is the Liberty Acorn Twenty, which is registered with Securities and Exchange Commission as a nondiversified fund and is managed by John Park. The SEC allows Park to put as much as a quarter of his fund's $271 million in assets in one stock, provided that he has no more than 5 percent of his remaining assets in any one security. Currently, Park has 58 percent of his assets in his top 10 holdings.

In down markets the performance of a fund with fewer stocks is less likely to be tied to the leading market indexes. The Liberty Acorn Twenty has a 9.8 percent total return by mid-2003 versus 6.7 percent for the S&P 500. For the past three years to date, the fund has a 10.6 percent annualized return compared to –11 percent for the S&P 500.

One trick that Park uses to reduce risk through diversification is to choose stocks that aren't correlated to each other, even if they're in the same industry. "Companies like Harley-Davidson and Liberty Media, though both lumped into the consumer category, don't trade in line with each other," says Park about two of his holdings. Such consumer-goods companies make up 14 percent of Park's portfolio.

Park says that an individual trying to build a concentrated portfolio would do well to not venture below $2 billion in market capitalization, to avoid liquidity risk, and to avoid companies that might be dependent on a small number of customers. He also recommends that investors pick low-debt companies with positive earnings over the last year. Park shoots for a three- to five-year time horizon on his investments.

But be disciplined about selling. Sometimes, a good pick will take off faster than anticipated. In a concentrated portfolio, an investment that posts a large price gain can easily grow to become too large a part of the whole. For example, in the middle of 2001 Park bailed out of medical equipment maker Boston Scientific, which he bought at an average price of $15 during the previous year, but which had climbed to $43. Now he favors Guidant, another medical equipment vendor.

Park warns that in any market, up or down, concentrated funds tend to be at both the top and bottom of the performance heaps. But the rewards are tantalizing. Berkshire Hathaway, a company with holdings in varied industries such as insurance and energy, is basically a concentrated fund, and the Sequoia Fund, started by protégés of Warren Buffett 33 years ago, has consistently trounced the broader market.

The Dividend Law

The dividend law says that whenever the dividend yield on the S&P 500 drops below 3 percent, it's a bad time to buy stocks. Unfortunately, we have left the days of the dividend behind, and it seems like they will never return. So dividend-based market valuations are no longer so relevant.

Consider that in the early days of the stock market, through the 1950s, many stock investors bought for dividends as much as they did for capital appreciation. Some stocks paid 10 percent of their share prices every year and some paid more. The dividend yield of a stock is the annual dividend divided by the stock price and expressed as a percentage. Obviously, if a company raises its dividend, and if the stock price stays the same, the yield will increase. If a stock price falls and the dividend remains constant, the yield will also increase. Because stock prices are far more volatile than dividends, the yield is largely price-dependent.

During the 1990s, stock prices soared while dividends stayed the same or were cut. Companies seemed to prefer to hang onto their cash or to use it to expand their businesses. Investors, faced with a choice between double-digit capital gains or a payout between 1 and 3 percent of their investment over the course of a year, sided with management. Companies also decided to use their cash to buy back their own shares on the open market. This buyback meant that they could pay their executives in options that would otherwise dilute shareholder's equity; they could then support their lofty stock prices. The cynical among you might note that the use of share buybacks to support high stock prices also greatly benefited those executives with their options.

In any event, share buybacks became and still are the preferred method of giving money back to the shareholders. That means that dividends have been cut while prices have risen and that the dividend yield has been permanently depressed. Even after the market shakeout, the dividend yield on the S&P 500 stands at just 1.75 percent, and it isn't likely to edge higher.

Investors who rely on the once tried-and-true dividend law will find that it no longer applies. For the S&P yield to rise to 3 percent, the market would either have to crash once more or companies would have to open their coffers to investors. Neither event is likely to occur, which means that the adherents of this notion will be left on the sidelines for a very long time.

You Can't Go Broke Taking a Profit

This is another one of those sayings that's meant to save investors from hanging on to a climbing stock that becomes a falling stock. With self-control and discipline, an investor can make a lot of money by taking small, substantial gains that add up over the life of a diversified portfolio. It's all just paper wealth until profits are taken. But be careful with this maxim, because it's just not true.

Say that you own a stock that's up $7 for the year and another that's down $9. Taking the $7 profit still leaves you down by $2. Every portfolio will have winners and losers, but the winners have to win by a wider margin than the losers lose. Sure, that's simple-minded advice, but investors often spend a lot of time looking at individual positions and not enough on the entire portfolio.

Besides, it isn't that simple, because you can't forget the government. If you hold on to your shares for at least two years, you pay a 15 percent tax in capital gains. If you hold for the short term, you pay at your personal income rate, which could be 35 percent. Obviously, if you are paying taxes, then you made a profit. But the after-tax profit has to beat the portfolio's losers in order for any money to be made, unless you plan to unload the losers in order to alleviate the tax burden.

You can also go broke taking a profit because investing isn't free. Say you are using a discount broker and you have just bought 100 shares of ABC Corporation. For the trade, you paid $14.95. That fee amounts to 15 cents per share. But that's only half the cost. Selling the shares will cost money too. If you want to unload all 100 shares at the same time, it will run you another 15 cents per share. That means you can't really sell at a profit until ABC shares gain more than 30 cents. If ABC is a large-cap stock, a 30-cent move might not be hard to find over the course of a few months. But if ABC is a smaller stock, 30 cents could amount to a large or unlikely percentage gain.

Mutual funds work the same way. If you invest in a load-bearing mutual fund and pay the sales charge up-front, then you really can't sell your shares in the fund until you've made up the 5.75 percent of assets you gave up to buy the fund. You have also got to worry about the management fee, probably around 1 percent, if you paid a sales charge. If you find a fund without a load, your odds of making a profit are better, because you only have to beat the 1.4 percent management fee you will probably be charged. Of course, this is an argument for buying low-cost mutual funds that don't have a sales charge. The point to remember is that profit counting doesn't begin until fee counting ends.

Most advisers believe that a portfolio of between 20 and 50 stocks is sufficient to supply adequate diversification without duplicating the market. Even big index funds that strive to duplicate market returns don't need every stock out there to do it. The Vanguard Total Stock Market Index Fund owns only about 3500 stocks, but it still very closely tracks the Wilshire 5000 Index. Doing so is possible because most indexes are weighted by market capitalization, owning more shares of the larger stocks. Because those stocks drive the overall performance, owning all of the smaller stocks isn't necessary. The problem for individual investors out for superior return is that they can inadvertently duplicate the market by owning too many of those market-moving stocks.

Buy the Whole Market

Why bother trying to beat the market? It's a legitimate question, given that most investors will fail. Buying the entire stock market and gaining exposure to companies of all sizes is cheap and easy these days, thanks to Vanguard's Total Stock Market Index Fund, which charges just $0.20 for every $100 invested. This is a great strategy for people who believe that their stock- or fund-picking skills will never beat the returns offered by the stock market over the long haul. Since Vanguard launched its first [S&P] 500 Index Fund in 1976, about a third of the managed funds in existence have managed to beat the index. That's not bad, but the odds are still against the investor. So buying the whole market through an index fund is not only cheap and easy, but it plays the odds since most people won't be able to match, let alone beat, the market's return.

But buying the entire market in a single index fund is not necessarily the best way to own the market. Craig Israelsen, a professor of consumer economics at the University of Missouri at Columbia, says you can index invest to a superior return. His complaint against the Vanguard Total Stock Market Index Fund is that it's weighted by market capitalization. This means that it owns more large-cap stocks than it does small caps. So that the price performance of a major manufacturing company like 3M will have a much greater effect on the total return than the price performance of a tiny biotech outfit in northern California. The smaller stocks, says Israelsen, have barely any effect at all on the Total Stock Market Index return, so Vanguard's product is really just an S&P 500 fund with a little taste of smaller stocks thrown in.

Israelsen would rather have his money equally spread among small-, mid-, and large-cap stocks. Instead of investing in the Vanguard Total Stock Market Index Fund, Israelsen recommends buying three index funds: the Vanguard Small-Cap Index, the Dreyfus MidCap Index, and the Vanguard 500 Index. Investing this way will expose you equally to small-, mid-, and large-cap stocks. Since the Vanguard Total Stock Market Index Fund is weighted by market value, its performance is dominated by the big blue chips. Between 1993 and the end of 2002, Israelsen's funds netted a 9.6 percent gain, which is a full point better than the Vanguard Total Stock Market Index Fund, after fees. That's not an enormous advantage but it can add up over time.

Whatever strategy you choose for owning the market, it's important to be careful about fund selection. An index fund should be cheap because the manager simply doesn't have that much to do. Some of the better managers like Vanguard's Gus Sauter at the Vanguard 500 Index Fund, will use index futures in order to keep transaction costs low. This means that Vanguard can charge less to its investors and bring home a superior return to boot. An index fund should never charge a sales load and should never charge more than $0.50 for $100 in assets. Beware: Morgan Stanley has a broker-sold index fund that costs 5.75 percent to buy and then $0.69 for every $100 under management. The old saying goes that some products aren't bought, they are sold. But the point of buying the entire market in an index fund is that it's cheap and easy and it's always easy to find a cheap index fund. So don't take a broker's first offer.

Buy the Dips

Every investor who's ever seen a stock chart knows that the market often rises after it falls. By all means, buy low and sell high, if you can. The phrase "buy the dips" is often spewed from the mouths of television's financial commentators and it always seems like a great idea—in retrospect. It's always a day, a month, or a year later that a stock's up-and-down day-to-day price chart seems to show all of the trades that could have been made. There's nothing wrong with wanting to buy stocks when they're cheap in order to sell them when they are expensive. That, after all, is the entire point of the endeavor. The problem with this theory is that price is just one part of what makes a stock cheap.

Think about stock the way you'd think about a car. If I tried to sell you a used Jetta for $50,000, you'd laugh in my face. If I cut the price to $30,000, you'd still have reason to laugh, even if the car is cheaper than it was a few moments ago. The used Jetta just isn't worth $50,000, it isn't worth $30,000, and I'd be lucky as the seller to get $8000. At least, in this case, you know that I'm lowering the price because I'm desperate to sell you a car.

Day traders will often buy the dips in an attempt to make money from market corrections. They hope to find a stock that will be heading up that day, because even though the general trend will be upward, the day will be full of moments where the stock dips. Buying during those moments is a good way to make a few cents on a one-day trade. It seems like a lot of work for not a lot of gain. Even though, in the postboom market, there are people who make their livings day trading their own money, I tend to doubt that the reward is worth the risk. Back in 1999 I profiled such a day trader for *Forbes* magazine. He specialized in buying the dips at the second they started to turn upward. The man boasted of earning a six-figure salary and only having to work for a few hours in the morning and a few hours in the afternoon. It sounded great, I thought—until my editor pointed out that if he had a job trading for Goldman Sachs, he'd be making far more than that. He'd also be risking none of his old money, also for about the same amount of work. Back then, the market only climbed. I have no idea how that day trader is doing now, but I bet he's having a tougher time of it. Day trading is a dangerous activity, no matter what the strategy.

But long-term investors try to do this as well, using charts that span weeks or months, again counting on a general stock trend to eventually carry the day as they jump on board, buying shares a bit cheaper than they'd normally be able to. So long as the investor has a reason for buying a stock and expecting it to appreciate over time, buying the dips long term makes a good deal of sense. Sometimes the market is temporarily wrong; that's how investors make money. Brief market downturns certainly create buying opportunities, and investors should keep an eye out for them.

It's important to remember that lines on a chart are nothing more than a representation of recent history and that they don't say anything about the future. A line that's going down can go down forever. Or it could head sideways or start climbing without warning. It's true that stock market corrections tend not to turn into prolonged bear markets. (These things happen two to three times a week during bull markets.) But don't forget that fundamentals move the market and that lines and graphs are only illustrations.

Buy the Rumor, Sell the Fact

This is an especially appealing myth because it implies that the investor, privy to the hottest and most important rumors that move the markets, has attained some special position within the financial world. It flatters the ego to imagine that you can hear about and properly determine which rumors are important and which are just noise. But it's almost always a mistake to assume, when you are one among a community of millions, that you enjoy some special status.

This old adage has more meaning for traders than for investors. Traders especially like to apply this principle when they get wind of an impending merger or acquisition. All of the speculation around such deals tends to create a lot of volatility in a stock and a runup in price that often ends as soon as the company makes an official announcement. Any corporate event can be used to employ this strategy, so long as the news is important enough to get other traders interested: the firing of a chief executive, a new product developed by a biotech firm, the closing or opening of a new manufacturing plant, and so on.

The hope for this kind of investor is that the market will like the rumor and the stock price will go up. Then, when the news confirms the rumor, the price will go higher and an investor could sell at a profit. Of course, everyone can't do this, because if they did, stock prices would jump on rumors and plummet on the news.

Of course, the biggest risk is that an investor will act on false rumors. The first step in verifying a rumor is to figure out its source. These days, after the Securities and Exchange Commission's Regulation: Fair Disclosure (RegFD), good rumors are hard to come by. Companies that plan to release material information about their operations are supposed to let everyone in the press and all of their analysts know the information at once so that nobody has an advantage. Of course, there are leaks in any organization, and sometimes rumors are planted for a reason. But leakers now face the threat of legal action from the SEC, if they are caught, so tones are more muted now than they have ever been.

Quality of rumor is a tough thing to discern. A few months ago a friend of mine who's a social worker told my wife that Eli Lilly would be coming out with a drug, aimed at the adult market, for treating attention deficit disorder, or ADD. He said it would be a great investment opportunity. As he saw it, the adults-with-ADD market has been so far untapped, despite the fact that professionals have been diagnosing adults with the illness. This is a pretty classic stock tip: A health professional lets two laypeople know about the intentions of a big drug company. As a tip or rumor, it is perfectly reasonable. But there's just one problem: The market didn't notice this at all. When Eli Lilly came out with the product, the stock actually moved down on other news. Had I bought Eli Lilly on that particular rumor and sold it on the uneventful news, I'd have surely lost money.

In that case, at least, all of the information was correct. The advent of Internet stock message boards in the late 1990s led to countless examples of phony rumors and even faked corporate press releases, mostly aimed at tiny stocks. Most people have become rightly skeptical of information presented in Internet forums and nowhere else. But it should also be noted that it's a bad idea to ever invest in a small-cap company based on a rumor. These companies are generally outside of the mainstream media's purview. So scam artists tend to believe that investors will have a hard time figuring out if rumors about such companies are false or true. Since small-cap companies are also traded thinly, a few people acting on phony information (or in concert, to make the phony tip seem true) can easily move the stock price. Scam artists are also less fearful of telling lies about small companies that might not have the money to pursue a legal claim against the liar. Not only can Microsoft's vast public relations machine dispel lies quickly, its vast team of lawyers can ruin the liar.

In an age where even a company's SEC filings are greeted by investors with skepticism, it would seem prudent to be wary of rumors and to invest on the merits of fact.

Buy and Hold

Investors convinced that the stock market offers long-term positive returns that beat cash and bonds are often tempted by the buy-and-hold approach. Investors with shorter time horizons or who get a thrill out of making rapid trades are convinced that they can beat it. These days, the latter class of investors are more common than the former.

The buy-and-hold theory of investing says it's best to build a diversified portfolio that can grow, with few changes, for decades. This is one of the most often-talked about topics in investing, but it's also one of the least believed. In the 1990s, the average holding period for stocks dropped from 28 months to 16. Mutual fund investors used to stay in their funds for over five years and now they stay in for less than three.

This is terrible news for investors. Investors who put $1000 in the market in 1980 and did nothing had over $16,000 in their accounts by the end of 2000. But investors who traded 85 percent of their shares (a figure matched by most mutual fund managers) wound up with just $8100 because of taxes and trading costs.

Investors have to endure immense pressure to trade. Most of it comes from their brokers, who make their money on trading fees that range between $15 and $30 a pop. One tool in the broker's arsenal is the myriad of analysts' reports that are published every quarter, touting new stocks and new sectors. The news media is constantly trumpeting new trends and touting new stock issues and new investment vehicles. An investor who has chosen to let the money work on its own feels left out of the game. But the real winners in all of this are brokerage houses and trading firms as surely as the casino is the real winner after every night of gambling.

The government also benefits from quick trades. Hold a security for more than two years and it is taxed at the 15 percent long-term capital gains rate. Sell it before then and it's taxed at the investor's income tax level, which can be as high as 35 percent.

This isn't to say that an investor should do absolutely nothing after entering the market. One flaw with the buy-and-hold approach is that it fails to acknowledge that people sometimes need their money. Investments aren't made because it's pretty to watch numbers grow over time. But when cashing out in order to put money to use or to rebalance the portfolio, consider selling losers instead of winners because they can be used to offset taxes. If you must sell winners, only sell those that are truly overvalued.

Know your personality. If you can't look at something without fiddling with it, try to only check on your portfolio, in detail, once a quarter. Also, set trading limits. Allow for, say, no more than 10 percent of the portfolio to be turned over in a given year.

Wall Street is an industry like any other, and it wants to sell you products and services. On any day of the year, a broker can give you a hundred reasons for dropping one stock in favor of buying another. Just remember that in the long run most insights about a company's present circumstances and future prospects are forgotten like so much other small talk. If enough thought went into the initial purchase of a stock, the topic won't need to be discussed too often in the following months.

Bulls and Bears Make Money, but Pigs Get Slaughtered

Most investors believe in healthy greed, and it seems like even people who haven't seen the Oliver Stone movie *Wall Street* know that Gordon Gecko says that "greed is good." But this old chestnut warns us that we can get too greedy, whether we are long or short on the market. Casinos make money because we tend to believe in things like "luck" and "streaks." But winning five spins of the roulette wheel doesn't change the odds at all for the sixth spin. Our impulse to "let it ride" when things are going our way is just a method of returning money to the house. Of course, most people enter a casino expecting to lose money. But in the stock market, investors tend to expect big winnings.

During the beginning of the 2000 bear market, the Institute of Psychology & Financial Markets released a study that said that one in five investors expect to get better than 20 percent a year in returns from stock investments. Vanguard founder John Bogle countered with a bit of reality, calling an 8 percent return realistic, with about 1 percent of that coming from dividends. An investor expecting to make 20 percent is bound to be disappointed by reality, and that disappointment can inspire bad decisions.

One common investor reaction, when confronted with returns that don't meet expectations, is to overreact and spend a lot of money trading old positions for new ones. This maneuver seldom does anything for returns, because even if the new stocks are better, the cost of buying them will wipe out the advantage. It's important to be patient and not to panic at the sight of a reasonable return.

Investors on a winning streak are also at risk. There's a tendency to equate stock market proficiency with genius. That's dangerous in a game where the only thing that distinguishes real skill from luck is a long track record. A stock on a roll can be infectious because it seems like it will climb forever. That's why it's important to check in on high-flying stocks every now and then and to make sure that the rise in price isn't completely out of proportion to the company's growth in sales or earnings. If it is, sell it. If it will pain you to watch the stock go up more after it's sold, then force yourself not to type its ticker into a Web site ever again.

Bulls believe that the market is going up, and bears believe it's going down. Pigs believe that Wall Street is like the farmer with the slop bucket, on his way to pour vast amounts of money into a trough. But really, the only greed that is consistent is the greed of Wall Street professionals. Stock prices rise and fall, but brokers always get their fees.

By all means, invest to become rich. But don't expect the money all at once.

Buy When There Is Blood on the Street

This is another strategy that flatters the investor. While everyone else is panicked or destroyed, the investor heroically walks the battlefield, looting from the foolish dead. The saying "buy when there is blood on the street" dates back to the legendary investor Lord Rothschild, who uttered the words on the eve of the Battle of Waterloo, when Napoleon's forces met their end at the hands of the British General Wellington.

Of course, the saying has nothing to do with war, especially as it's used today. It's actually just another way of telling investors to buy stocks at their bottoms, or to buy the whole market at the bottom. There's nothing wrong with that. If you have an especially acute sense of when the market has bottomed, and you're right in all cases, then by all means buy at the bottom. The problem is, you can spend an entire life investing and even investing well, without ever once correctly calling the bottom of the market.

Between 1929 and 1954, the Dow fell from a high of 386 to a low of 40—a 90 percent decline. No doubt, had you been able to buy shares when the Dow was at 40 and then held them until 1954, when the Dow reached its high again, you'd have enjoyed a whopping 865 percent return. But how would you have known to wait that long? Remember, the Dow fell by 90 percent. A drop in the Dow to 200, which would have been a 48 percent decline, might have seemed plenty bloody to me. But at that point, the market was set to fall another 160 points.

More recently, certain indexes like the technology-heavy Nasdaq have undergone bloody years. It's up 20 percent so far in 2003, but that's to just over 1600. The index pushed 5000 in the year 2000. At that level, the Nasdaq at 3000 was fairly bloody, and the Nasdaq at 2300 was extremely bloody. So congratulations if you decided to jump back into the Nasdaq at just under 1300. But that's just not the kind of luck you will be able to count on happening again.

This bloody logic could also be applied to individual stocks that have their own bloody moments from time to time. Sometimes value stocks are made this way, and in the contrarian tradition of Benjamin Graham, the fact that a company has become unpopular is always a good reason to have a look at it. But be careful. A little blood is one thing, but a gushing wound is another.

This myth is, of course, similar to "buy the dips," and it is another cousin to "buy low, sell high." That's what everybody's trying to do. Best of luck to you.

Bear Markets Last About a Year

We'd all like to believe that there's some sort of limit on how long a market can stay in bearish territory. Since the markets are just the culmination of desires among traders throughout the world, it seems logical that there would be some limit. Also, we know that the stock market is a safe place for capital and offers positive returns over the long run, so it must be true that bull markets are either more frequent than bear markets or have greater impact. Since some analysts claim that all the time between 1982 and 2000 was a bull market, it seems safe to say that bear markets are indeed a short-term phenomenon. But do they really tend to last a year?

We're presently in a bear market that seems to be breaking during its third year, so that's evidence against the notion right there. But no matter what happens to the current bear market (which seems to be heading back toward hibernation even as I type), we can also see that there have been bearish periods in the stock market that have lasted as long as the great bull run of 1982. Between 1906 and 1921, stocks lost money. The time between 1929 and 1934 was another rotten period for the long-term investor. From 1968 through 1982, the market betrayed our hopes.

Of course, markets are volatile, and there was money to be made during all of those bearish periods. In 1930, for example, there was a midyear price recovery where folks made money. The years between 1968 and 1982 were awful, but the months between the beginning of 1968 and the tail end of 1969 weren't so nasty.

In light of this data, stretching back to the start of the twentieth century, it seems that bears were out for a third of the century. Andrew Smithers and Stephen Wright, in their book *Valuing Wall Street*, take issue with the notion of long-term buy-and-hold investing because of these frequent bear visits. I'm using their data to make the point that bear markets aren't so short-lived as we think. I'll also borrow a bit of their insight to reconcile these revelations with the modern investor's knowledge that stocks offer positive, long-term returns. Smithers and Wright argue that if you look at the chart of stock prices from 1950 onward, the long-term theory really bears fruit. Add the 50 years you cut off and it seems like the markets can indeed be unforgiving for long periods of time. According to the Smithers and Wright data, most of those long-term gains really materialized with the great bull market of 1982.

It might be, of course, that the global economy and the behavior of the stock market are fundamentally different now than they were before 1950. Perhaps the country's increased financial strength and effective regulation of the securities industry will make it possible for long bull runs and brief bear sightings. Maybe the evolution of stock investing from an activity reserved for the privileged few to everyone in America has changed the game a bit as well. We all have a stake in the market, and we want it to do well; if the market is an expression of collective will, then it should do well. In an era where recessions have replaced depressions, perhaps the bad times don't last so long.

That's a nice thought, but I don't think it's true. There's always a chance, while confidence is shaken, for a long bear market, and there's no structural guarantee that it will end quickly. The good news is that careful stock and fund selection can generate profits even in a terrible market.

P A R T

2

Stock Picking

THE MARKET IS JUST a collection of stocks that investors can sift through. Just as the soothsayers utter their myths about the markets in general, they have a myriad of ideas about each and every stock and how to find them.

Follow a Few Stocks Well

There's no doubt that investors are overwhelmed with information these days. Spend an afternoon scrolling through the Yahoo! Finance Web pages. If you tried to pore through all of the news stories, the gossip on the message boards, the balance sheets, and the myriad of SEC filings available, you'd be lucky to get through five companies. You'd be even luckier to remember what you learned a few hours later. Since most investors aren't professional analysts and haven't quit their day jobs, even finding an afternoon for such Herculean research is a problem. Still, though the homework is hard, it is a necessary part of investing. Limiting the amount of stocks in which you are interested is a good way to make sure that your research is diligent.

Don't worry so much about diversification. You can always diversify instantly by putting some money in a low-cost S&P 500 index fund, or you could buy shares of an exchange-traded fund that tracks the broader stock market. The financial world is rife with products that offer exposure to the total market, just don't pay too much for them. Then, pick stocks that will help your portfolio beat the market.

Wall Street professionals always limit their scope. Analysts at the major brokerage houses usually follow just one sector, and then they cover between 5 and 10 companies, usually using assistants to help them with the workload. Mutual funds that have a wide array of holdings often rely on staffs of analysts who are also deployed to study the market on a sector-by-sector basis.

Some of the best money managers on Wall Street are also specialists in just a few stocks. Consider the Sequoia Fund, managed by William Ruane and Robert Goldfarb. Over the last five years it has beaten the S&P by 6 percent, and it has 15 stock holdings in its $4 billion portfolio. The fund's largest position, a $1.3 billion stake in Berkshire Hathaway, makes up a third of the portfolio, and 96 percent of Sequoia's money is in just 10 stocks. We'll discuss the dangers of overdiversification and the value of a concentrated portfolio in the chapter entitled "Don't Overdiversify." Here, the example of

Sequoia only serves to show that highly successful, professional money managers don't pretend that they can know it all.

Once investors have narrowed their scope, they need to figure out what information to follow. Especially in the technology and biotech sectors, it's impossible for the lay investor to entirely understand the product that a company manufactures. Knowing that desktop computers are important and that the company you are researching makes them reliably and with better profit margins than the competition is important. Knowing how to build a computer out of its component parts isn't.

Because no company is an island, it's important to gain some familiarity with a company's industry sector. A good stock should trade more cheaply than others in the sector, have a clean balance sheet, have a product that is either superior to or more cheaply manufactured than the competition, and be gaining market share to rivals. Most brokerage houses offer industry sector reports that can be a good source of this type of information.

It's also important to know a bit about a company's major customers. A server manufacturer like Cisco will live or die by the performance of its corporate clients, especially Web-based companies. Some smaller companies that make equipment for corporate clients derive most of their revenue from two or three customers. If that company is still a favorite, then it's imperative that you know its customers are healthy and tied into long-term contracts with your potential investment. Companies that primarily sell products to other businesses will thus demand a bit more research than companies that sell directly to individual consumers.

But on the consumer side, it's important not to be so myopic that you miss the rise of a new competitor that might take you and your investment down a peg or two.

To thoroughly research even one potential investment might mean building at least a familiarity with 3 to 10 other companies that are either in the sector or that depend on the sector.

But you will never know them all. So stay diligent and stay on target.

Being a Good Company Doesn't Mean Being a Good Stock

Were it true that every company with solid earnings, a good track record, and a stellar management team were immediately rewarded by the market then there would be no way to pick stocks destined to outperform. A certain amount of market ignorance is the friend of any stock picker. It's also possible for a company to have everything going in its favor and for its stock to languish in spite of its good story. Among those investors more enamored of ticker symbols than company names, you will frequently hear that a good company isn't necessarily a good stock. In the short term, the market doesn't necessarily care who's on a company's management team or what the long-term sales growth looks like. Short-term investors look for stocks that will be immediately rewarded by the market, so they tend not to think in terms of good and bad companies. Some more analytical investors find good companies with stagnant stocks and ignore them in the hopes that some "catalyst" in the form of a new-product launch or news even will get the stock moving again. Of course, investing before the catalyst occurs, not after, makes the real money.

Even a cursory glance at recent financial history proves that the reverse of this hypothesis, that bad companies make for bad stocks, is undeniable.

First, we have the companies like Enron, WorldCom, and HealthSouth, which were done in by fraud. A great stock, it seems, does not necessarily represent a great company. During the technology boom, the market was full of great stocks. Webvan was once a stock picker's dream. The company went public at $15 and more than doubled in price during its first month. It was a great stock. But it wasn't a great company. At its core, Webvan provided services that most people don't need because our society has not yet become so lazy that we can't drive a few blocks to get our groceries ourselves. (Besides, most grocery stores can undercut a company like Webvan by offering in-house delivery services.) Webvan had debt, no earnings, and a great stock—for a while. The stock is worth nothing now.

Good companies do make for good stocks, in the long run. But what do we mean by good companies? First, they have to sell a product that people want. They have to show positive earnings, have consistent revenue growth, and hold a reasonable amount of debt. Assets, defined by book value, are a big plus. What makes a good company good depends largely on a company's industry and how it stacks up, on a fundamental basis, relative to its peers. The question "what is a good company?" is, of course, as subjective as the question "what is a good movie?" Still, there are certain things that most good movies have in common: decent production values, a strong cast, and an engaging, linear story.

Good companies are also defined by the quality and honesty of management. In March 2001, professor Bernard Black of the Stanford Law School, examined firms in Russia to see if good corporate governance (issuing transparent financial releases, respecting rights for shareholders, and having honest managers) translated into market success. He chose Russia because its market is depressed due to a lack of investor confidence in its firms and in regulatory control. As a financial market, Russia is still tainted by the specter of financial oligarchs who took control as Russian President Boris Yeltsin sought to bring the country into the capitalist global economy. Russia is just now emerging from an age of robber barons that is reminiscent of American capitalism in the nineteenth century. But Russia, in sore need of foreign investment capital, will have to develop more quickly than the United States did. According to Black, the Russian stock market has a potential value of $3 trillion. But because investors have no reason to trust that corporate insiders at Russian companies won't loot and skim for themselves, the entire universe of Russian stocks is worth just $30 billion.

Black used a corporate governance ranking developed by the Brunswick Warburg investment bank, which examined the charters of major Russian corporations. The bank was looking for regulations that barred insider trading or called for the presence of board members who are independent of the company's management. He also analyzed the companies for their assets, sales, and growth, to determine what they would be worth if they were American companies, trading under U.S. rules. The Russian firm Lukoil, for example, would be worth $195 million in the U.S. market. It's worth just $5.5 million in Russia. It's also ranked 20 on the corporate governance scale. Compare that with a company like Vimplecom, a Russian telephone company that's ranked 7 on corporate governance—it's trading at about half of its potential U.S. market cap. The results of Black's study: The better a company is governed, the smaller the gap between its Russian and U.S. value. Shareholders will pay a premium, it seems, for good companies.

Never Fall in Love with Horses or Stocks

Investing is a process of choosing favorites. To put money into one stock rather than another is to bet on a belief in a stock's superiority, and that means believing in a company's products, business model, prospects, and management. The companies themselves, in an effort to attract investors and customers, are in constant sales mode and are trying to remain always appealing and likable. It has worked to an often ludicrous extent. During the late 1990s, for example, investors referred to Microsoft by the cutesy nickname "Mister Softee," as if its stock had become a return-generating substitute for the trusty stuffed animals of childhood. That's love, and it's never healthy.

It's already been established elsewhere in this book that patience is a weapon in an investor's arsenal and that keeping a low-turnover portfolio is a great way to reduce brokerage costs, increase tax efficiency, and make money in the long run. But it should also be said that the investor owes nothing to the investment.

Sometimes, for example, a stock can pay off too well and become overvalued as its price increases. Those stocks need to be sold. It's always difficult to part with winners, but when a stock's price has gone through the roof, its circumstances have changed and the position has to be at least reevaluated.

Another problem with the great performers is that they can throw a portfolio out of balance. Particularly after spin-offs and mergers, and sometimes after stock splits, one good stock might wind up representing 50 percent of the value in a portfolio. In that case, success has led to a lack of diversification. It might be a good idea to sell off some of that position to get exposure to other sectors and companies within the market. My aunt Bella, for example, worked as an operator for Ma Bell for almost all of her life, and the company gave her a certain amount of stock. When the government broke up its monopoly, she wound up with shares of AT&T and all of the Baby Bells that were created. Then she wound up with shares of companies like Lucent. Not much interested in the stock market, she tended to follow a strategy of selling shares when the names of companies got too weird and high-tech sounding. That worked well enough for her but she also had a solid pension to rely on. Today's generation of future retirees will want to diversify more carefully, as recent history has shown that a portfolio made up entirely of telecom stocks, even if it all came from a few stock gifts earlier in the century, just isn't the safest way to invest.

The above situations, involving rapid price appreciation are problems that every investor should love to have. But investors may also have to deal with other, unhappy scenarios. Sometimes the world changes and good companies go under.

Employees of public companies tend to make particularly loyal investors. When Enron collapsed due to the actions of its executives, many of its employees were destroyed with the company. They were happy, while the stock was on the rise, to load Enron shares into their 401(k) plans. When the news turned sour, those employees were prevented from unloading their shares because of various restrictions imposed on employee stock trades. Enron might have been a great place to work, but that should have been no reason to count on its stock, on its own, to fund the retirement years. The company you work for is probably the company you know the best, so owning some of the stock (if you subject it to the same rigorous analysis you'd perform on any other stock) might be a good idea. But investors should also consider their salaries as part of their investment portfolios. If you already get $50,000 a year from your company, maybe you don't need much more exposure to it in the form of the company's stock.

There are also fairly legendary companies with names that are well known and are likable because they are indelibly part of the history of American industry. Owens Corning is a solid fiberglass manufacturing company that started business in 1935. It has 20,000 employees and sales of $5 billion a year. The stock first went public back in 1952, just as a long bear market was about to give way. But it currently trades at $0.63 a share and is reorganizing its balance sheet under the supervision of a bankruptcy court. No doubt it has been a good company with a long pedigree and an important part of American industry. It also has asbestos liabilities and has thus become a target for lawsuits. Now, investors will argue around and around, based usually on their politics, about the merits of those lawsuits. Nevertheless, the lawsuits exist, and they have changed the fortunes of Owens Corning. No amount of love for the stock or the company could have prevented that.

Finally, beware the cult of personality. Magazine cover stories, television news, and the business book publishing industry tend to build up certain managers and innovators as heroes. That's fine, because those hero stories make for good airplane reading. But these titans of industry, who seem like they just stepped out of the pages of an Ayn Rand novel, aren't flawless super-beings. Consider Al "Chainsaw" Dunlap. He had a colorful background as a West Point graduate and Army paratrooper, and he earned his nickname when he took over the struggling Scott Paper Company and laid off 11,000 workers. He also negotiated more favorable contracts with Scott's suppliers and created a lean operation that was sold to Kimberly Clark for $6.5 billion. He might not have had a soft touch, but in the Scott situation, he turned a company flirting with bankruptcy into a multibillion-dollar acquisition target.

Dunlap became a celebrity CEO—such a celebrity, in fact, that in 1998 he was courted to take over another troubled company called Sunbeam. He bought Sunbeam stock at $12 a share before his new assignment began. When it was announced to Wall Street that "The Chainsaw" was going to start cutting into Sunbeam, the stock jumped to $17 a share. But Dunlap's tenure was, to say the least, troubled. The SEC accused him of accounting trickery, and investors followed with a lawsuit. Dunlap later settled all of this for $500,000 to the government and $15 million to Sunbeam investors. After Dunlap stepped down from the chief executive post, Sunbeam filed for bankruptcy protection in 2001, citing Dunlap's debt-financed acquisitions as one of the reasons. Then the company emerged as a private concern in late 2002. Investors expecting a boon from "Chainsaw" were left disappointed.

No company is perfect and no executive is perfect, so be vigilant when investing. Avoid cultishly following a stock or an individual.

As a Bull Market Begins to Peak,
Sell the Stock That Has Gone Up the Most—
It Will Drop the Fastest;
Sell the Stock That Has Gone Up the Least—
It Didn't Go Up, So It Must Go Down

The stock that rose the fastest in a bull market is generally worthy of some special attention, because it represents whatever fad most recently helped to drive the market. In 2000, technology stocks were at the end of a long ride up, and they were hammered hard on the way down. From that perspective, it's easy to see how investors would believe this maxim. The problem is in the application of the technique. Nobody really knows when a bear market is going to begin. The label "bear" or "bull" is applied months after the market exhibits the bearish or bullish behavior. The media and analysts can't call a trend, after all, until the trend has had time to develop.

Let's start at the beginning of a bull market. Most analysts will agree that the last great bull run began on August 12, 1982, when the Dow stood at 777. It ended, roughly, on the last day of March 2000. That's an 18-year run.

Of course, for every day of each of those 18 years, people said that the bull market had peaked, or was going to end, or was maybe about to end in a few months. But it didn't. Nothing was able to end it: not the crash of 1987, the Asian financial crises, the failure of the massive Long Term Capital Management hedge fund, nor military actions in Grenada, Panama, Iraq, and the former Yugoslavia.

In 2000, months before the crash, I profiled in *Forbes* magazine a fund manager who had been bearish on the market for over a decade. Of course, I was a bit snide about all of the money his investors had missed out on by ignoring the markets that were clearly rising around him. All those negative news and financial moments mentioned in the preceding paragraph weren't enough to keep this bear's returns positive. Of course, I got a call from the gentleman a few weeks after the market crashed (he's a true gentleman and actually waited a bit) asking what I thought of him now. Well, I figured, if you spend years predicting the end of the bull market, you're bound to be right at some point. His one shining moment might have come a few weeks after my article (curse the universe for its sense of humor), but it doesn't wipe away years of being wrong.

Nobody can predict the end of a bull market with any accuracy. Nobody. So if you have no idea when the market is going to peak, then you can't sell the stock that's gone up the most, because you'll never be sure about when to sell.

But, let's say you defy me and that you did manage to predict the end of the 1982 bull market. Most of the companies that went into free-fall when the bubble burst weren't even public in 1982. One highflier from the era, that went public in 1986, is Microsoft. It sold for a split-adjusted $0.07 a share. Now it trades at $24, and that's after another split. On a split-adjusted basis, the stock actually peaked in March 2000 at $28.75. So over the course of the bear market, the stock is still up. At it's lowest point, Microsoft traded at a split-adjusted $10 per share. That 58 percent decline between March and December of 2000 is a pretty hefty drop, but the stock certainly didn't give back all of its bull market gains. It didn't even come close. Had you sold it, you would have really missed out, because two years after the bear market, Microsoft had actually climbed back to its bubble price and then the stock was split. A lot of other companies out there never recovered.

Never Try to Catch a Falling Knife

Know yourself before you decide whether or not to ignore this old Wall Street saw. Some stocks do indeed fall all the way into bankruptcy, never to emerge. Webvan, an Internet delivery company that sought to free the nation from ever having to leave their couches for groceries and consumer goods, was valued at $4.8 billion a month to the day before the Nasdaq crash in March 2000. Once it started dropping, it dropped to zero. Buying Webvan on its dip was a suicide dive.

A company needn't go bankrupt just to never relive its highs. Internet retailer Amazon.com, still in business and likely to remain so for a long time, will likely never reach its tech bubble price of $600 a share. There were plenty of opportunities to buy Amazon on the way down and still lose money.

Still, all of the great value investors like Benjamin Graham and Warren Buffett have made money by buying unpopular stocks, and a sharp price decline is a good sign of a stock's unpopularity. For an investor who can discern the difference between a stock that's out of favor and a stock that's out of time, catching falling knives is like catching falling money. Charles Brandes, a San Diego–based money manager with $60 billion portfolio under management, recently directed his researchers to look into the "falling knives" phenomena.

Brandes's firm examined the fate of 1000 companies that had lost 60 percent of their market value within a 12-month period between 1986 and the end of 2002. They struck penny stocks from the study by requiring that each company have a market cap of $100 million. Within three years of their precipitous declines, 13 percent of the firms were in bankruptcy. But despite those failures, the Brandes portfolio of losers actually gained 35 percent in the first year after the drop-off and 18 percent over three years.

Brandes's conclusion: "An investment strategy that contemplates owning 'falling knives' may indeed leave the manager holding 'the next Enron,' but our study suggests that—particularly in a portfolio context—this approach may improve aggregate portfolio returns over time."

The key to the strategy is that it's a portfolio. Catching one falling knife seems like a good way to lose a finger. But catching a bunch of them is a way to capitalize on the notion that downtrodden stocks will outperform market favorites that have little upside left.

Obviously, an investor needs some stomach for risk in order to follow this model. There's bankruptcy risk involved. If you'd invested alongside the Brandes study as it progressed, 130 companies in your portfolio would have fallen into bankruptcy. As investors, we're taught to avoid this at all costs. But these losses have to be taken in perspective of the total portfolio. Sure, professional money managers, especially mutual fund managers, spent a lot of time explaining why they owned stocks like Enron, World-Com, and Conseco, but those were really "news of the day" questions. In the end, overall performance is what matters.

In the search for overall performance through a diversified portfolio of stocks, bankruptcy is a real risk that investors have to face. Every investor has failed, every investor has held a company that they just don't want to talk about at parties. But not having owned WorldCom is nothing to brag about when the whole portfolio's lagging the market. The most useful lesson from the Brandes Institute study is that a portfolio can take a few bankruptcies and still finish in positive territory.

The caveat is that most investors don't and won't own 1000 individual stocks. If you are a rotten stock picker, choosing from among those companies that have fallen 60 percent in a year might be a disaster. One thing to guard against is liquidity risk. Remember, you don't have to hold these fallen stocks forever, and the ride might be more than you can stomach. The Brandes study has a $100 million cutoff, but as market caps grow, volume tends to grow and stocks are more liquid. At this writing, drug maker Bristol-Myers Squibb is a $43 billion company that has taken a beating. A sell order on this stock is unlikely to languish for days after your broker sends it on. The individual investor might only look at fallen angels with market caps of $400 million or more as they tend to be liquid stocks.

But forget the notion that any company is too big to fail. Enron was once an $80 billion company. Paper valuations are always ephemeral.

For the individual, fundamental analysis is indispensable. Companies with large stores of tangible assets, low debt (or an arrangement with creditors that will greatly reduce debt within two years), positive earnings, and good prospects are least likely to fail. With $60 billion at his disposal, Brandes can diversify to the point where bankruptcies can be soon forgotten. Most investors aren't so well endowed.

Share Buybacks Are a Sign of
Shareholder-Friendly Management

As a stockholder, you are part owner of a company that is run on your behalf by a management team that answers to a board of directors charged with looking out for your interests. Your stock makes you an owner of every part of the company. You own the factories, the retail outlets, the fleet of trucks, the corporate jet, the stocks on the corporate balance sheet, the cash in the bank, and the quarterly earnings.

Usually, stockholders don't make too big a deal about the corporate jet, but the money in the bank and the money rolling in? Well, that's why you bought a stake in the company, isn't it? Management has a few options for all that cash on its balance sheet: They can hoard it, use it to expand operations, distribute it to stockholders in the form of a dividend, or use it to bolster the company's stock price by buying back stock on the open market.

Both the dividend and the share buyback options are ways of giving money to investors. A dividend is a direct, quarterly payment to investors. A share buyback program helps to support the stock price out in the market by reducing supply. The announcement of such a program generally causes a company's stock to bounce temporarily, creating a good selling opportunity for investors looking to unload. That's the theory, anyway.

If management really has no other motivation than to distribute money to shareholders, then the dividend payment is the best method because it's direct, easy, and not subject to punitive taxation.

Management, of course, has other interests. The first is that most of the executive team is now paid in stock options which, when exercised, can cause an increase in the supply of stock on the market. The more stock there is, the less price pressure will come from demand. Worse, earnings metrics like the earnings per share will go down. More stock means that the earnings have to be spread out more thinly. That makes the company look bad on paper and will hurt stock performance in the long run. Buying back shares as options are exercised helps to keep earnings from being diluted.

That's a good thing, but these buybacks basically just allow management to collect more options for themselves with impunity.

Management can also make earnings per share look better by taking shares off the market. In the long run, this will make the company's stock look better. To new investors who want to buy a piece of the earnings, it's a good thing, because one share now buys more earnings. But to the growth investor, interested in the growth of earnings over time, it's confusing. The earnings growth caused by a share buyback is just a trick; it has nothing at all to do with the way the company is being run.

Andrew Smithers and Stephen Wright argue in *Valuing Wall Street* that corporate stock buying served to inflate the stock market as corporations became the most likely buyers of stock between 1993 and 1998. Indeed, Smithers and Wright show the American individual investor was actually a net seller of securities throughout that period and that corporations were snapping up what the individuals had left on the floor. Were it not for the corporations, say Smithers and Wright, the bull market of the 1990s might well have been a bear market.

Certainly, corporations buy stock for reasons other than share buybacks. Most corporations have investment portfolios, and many have in-house retirement plans that are fueled by investments. But Smithers and Wright classify share buybacks (some of which are actually financed by debt) and the growing popularity of issuing stock options to executives, as nothing more than a Ponzi scheme.

In the end, you should judge management the same way you'd judge yourself. If a company's stock is legitimately undervalued, then perhaps a buyback is a good idea. If a company is going to buy back pieces of itself, it should do so cheaply. The company should also use cash and not debt to finance such transactions. Finally, companies that don't pay dividends should do so before they start buying back stock.

Never Hold On to a Loser
Just to Collect the Dividends

Dividends are a tricky topic, because there are two ways of looking at them. The first is in terms of cash: What is the actual cash payout that a company promises on an annual or quarterly basis? The second is in terms of the dividend yield, which is the stock price divided by the dividend, expressed as a percentage—that tells the investor what guaranteed return is being promised. In a sense, it's always good when stocks pay dividends; it shows that management knows that the shareholders own the company and are thus entitled to the company's money. It also promises, for a time, a certain return. But, the return offered by capital appreciation will always outpace the return offered by dividends, so it's no good hanging on to a loser on the sole basis of dividends.

During the bear market, Vanguard founder John Bogle warned that investors shouldn't count on more than an 8 percent average annual return from the stock market once it recovers. He attributed just 1 percent of that return to dividends. Although 1 percent is nothing to sneeze at over time, it does show how little dividends seem to matter these days. Dividend yields are at an all-time low, as most management teams these days prefer to either hoard cash or to use it to make acquisitions.

Think about it this way: If the yield on a dividend paying stock is 1.75 percent, then it isn't really paying better than a good certificate of deposit at the bank or a money market fund. A 1.75 percent return can easily be matched without exposing yourself to any capital risk except from inflation. Companies have become so stingy about paying dividends that they should barely factor into stock selection. If you like a company, buy it, and if they pay a dividend, that's a treat.

To illustrate why a falling stock isn't worth hanging on to because of the dividend payout, let's discuss the dividend yield again. The equation is as follows:

$$\frac{\text{Annual dividend}}{\text{Price per share}} = \text{Dividend yield}$$

As with most of these price-based equations, the price part of it is the one that's going to change most often. As an unlikely example, say a $2 stock pays $1 a year. The dividend yield is 50 percent. If the price drops to $1, then the dividend yield is 100 percent. That scenario makes a great case for buying the stock at $1 because it means that by the end of the year, no matter what happens to the stock price, the investor will be made whole by collecting dividends. But an investor who bought at $2 doesn't benefit at all. The dividend yield at the time of purchase is the only one that really matters no matter what happens to the price. The only time an increasing dividend yield is good news for investors is when the dividend goes up. If the dividend yield falls because of price appreciation, that doesn't matter either. It's the initial investment that matters in terms of calculating the total return.

Dividends are wonderful when you can find them. A company that pays a dividend has cash in the bank and is likely to be a stable, ongoing concern for a long time. Dividend taxes have been reduced, and they represent an actual, tangible return. They can also be used to offset or reduce the impact of a broker's fee. If it costs $15 to invest $500, then you have paid 3 percent for the transaction. If you have invested in stocks offering a 3 percent dividend yield, you are no longer starting from negative territory.

One thing to watch out for: Companies can easily change the dividend payout, and shareholder opposition will usually not stop that change from happening. Management isn't bound to keep or increase a dividend program. Sometimes, a company that reduces dividends is signaling rough economic times ahead or admitting that it's short of cash. Other times, it signals a change in strategy. (The company might be heading into an acquisition mode.) In the short term, the market will generally punish companies that reduce or suspend dividend payments.

One advantage of dividends is that most companies have dividend reinvestment programs so that these payouts can be immediately converted into more stock. That's a good way to add to positions in sturdy and reliable companies.

Buy the Dogs of the Dow

As of this writing, the "Dogs of the Dow," defined as the 10 stocks in the Dow Jones Industrial Average that have the highest dividend yields, are paying an average 4.75 percent in dividends every year. That's more than 2 percentage points better than most money market funds, and it's a point and a half better than you will get out of 10-year U.S. Treasuries. So on dividend alone, at least at this point in history where interest rates are at historic lows and the stock market is depressed, buying the Dogs of the Dow seems like a good idea.

Yield aside, the dogs tend to be solid companies. Some of the dogs from 2003 include JPMorgan Chase, Exxon Mobil, Caterpillar, General Electric, and General Motors. No bankruptcy risk there, and solid companies all. Some of these are downright value stocks. Consider that Exxon Mobil trades for 16 times earnings while its peers in the oil exploration and production sectors are trading at an average 21 times earnings.

Neil Hennessy, manager of the Hennessy Balanced Fund, uses the Dogs of the Dow approach in managing his $15 million mutual fund. The strategy has worked reasonably well to keep him invested in solid companies. His portfolio has a price-to-earnings ratio of 25, which means that he's buying earnings at half the price of an S&P 500 fund. The average market cap of his stocks is $30 billion, confirming that the strategy leads to investments in big, solid companies. Because the fund is a mutual fund, and it is restricted from putting more than 5 percent of assets into any one company, Hennessy keeps half of his assets in cash. Net of fees, his returns have been modest. He's up 4 percent over 5 years, while the S&P 500 is up 6 percent and the Dow is up 7.5 percent. The exposure to big companies and cash helped him in 2002. He was off only 4.5 percent, while the S&P dropped 22 percent. Hennessy's performance, while not bad, isn't so great that it should convert anyone to the strategy. He even had the help of his cash positions to alleviate the trauma of down markets.

But given that the Dogs of the Dow strategy does seem like an effective way of finding stable companies that are trading cheaply, it might behoove

people to check out the list once a year. Slavish devotion to the Dogs investment style isn't worthwhile, but taking an occasional peek into the dog
pound to see if there's a puppy or two worth bringing home might be.

Investors who want to try the strategy should know that it calls for an
annual rebalancing, and the typical Dow of the Dogs investor will have to
replace three to four stock positions every year. That kind of turnover costs
money, both in taxes and brokerage fees that will eat into the overall return.

Buy the Stock That Splits

Companies split their stocks in order to make shares more affordable to investors. A two-for-one stock split has the result of cutting a stock's price in half. Many investors believe that after a split, the stock will soon climb back to its presplit levels. While such reasoning sounds nice, there's no reason for that statement to be true, based on the way that stocks are valued.

Remember that when a stock splits, all of the data associated with a share will split as well. If a company is trading at $50 and reporting $4 of earnings per share, it is trading at 12.5 times earnings. After a stock split, the shares will trade at $25 and earnings per share will drop to $2, which is still 12.5 times earnings. In February 2003, Microsoft announced a two-for-one stock split that brought its $48 stock down to $24. Six months later, the stock is still hovering at around $24 per share.

The only reason that a stock split would boost the stock price is that split stocks are more affordable on a price basis. Most investors would agree that Berkshire Hathaway is a well-run company. But few investors can afford to buy even one class A share in the company, which trades at around $16,000. That trade price is so high because Buffett has never split his stock. One share of Berkshire is about the size of a small investment portfolio.

But on a price-to-earnings basis, despite the high cost of its stock, Berkshire Hathaway is cheaper to buy than Microsoft. Berkshire trades at 22 times earnings. Microsoft's price is 27 times earnings. No amount of stock splitting will change that fundamental fact. A lot of individual investors would love to rush into Berkshire Hathaway were the stock to split to the point where it trades at $50 a share. Though that influx of new investor money might give a fleeting boost to Berkshire's stock price, the institutional investors who really know the market (and who don't have to balk at Berkshire's hefty price) won't view the stock any differently for splitting. That's why Microsoft after the split is worth the same as it was before the split: The market cares about value, not price.

Owning stocks that split can be good because the investor is given more shares in the company. Also, although the value of the stock on the day of the split would be unchanged, owning more shares could be beneficial in the future. Owning one share of ABC Corporation that goes up by $1 means there's a $1 gain. Owning two shares that go up by a dollar means there's a $2 gain. But that's only a boon to investors who already own the stock. Of course, per-share losses are also similarly compounded.

There's nothing wrong with stock splits, but there is also nothing to get excited about.

Buy on Weakness, Sell on Strength

This is the cousin maxim to the famous "buy low, sell high," but it's an easier rule to follow. While there's no way of knowing if a stock has reached its low or high point until after that point has already happened, it is fairly simple to look at a chart to see what direction a stock's price is pointing. But should you?

There's a class of investors out there who follow colored lines instead of companies. They are derisively known as "chartists," and they are not to be followed by the investor who values fundamental analysis. The problem with looking at a stock chart instead of a balance sheet is that a stock's price can change direction on a dime—actually, on a fraction of a penny. If investing were really as easy as reading fever charts, we'd all be rich and never do any real work.

But, there is something useful about this saying because we are hardwired to make the opposite mistake. When most investors see a stock in decline, they see a loser and they are glad they don't own it. We are drawn to winners. We are attracted to stocks that show upward motion on a graph. But if we chase Wall Street's winners and buy stocks as their prices go up, we are quite likely to find ourselves buying near or at the top of the market. Then, when the stock turns into a loser, we sell it. We do the opposite of buying low and selling high.

So while price charts are rotten stock-picking tools by themselves, they do have their place. Say you find a stock with a price that seems to be in decline. You check the balance sheet and find out that the company is a solid one. You check the news and make sure there is no scandal, impropriety, or major changes in business focus or management on the horizon. Everything is fine. It's just a classic case of a good stock being sold off. Then, maybe, if the stock is well valued relative to its industry peers on a price-to-earnings, price-to-sales, or price-to-book basis, you have got a value stock worth buying. But remember, a stock in decline can continue declining.

If that happens, consider selling for a tax loss to offset better-planned decisions. While some investors will sit on paper losses forever, in the hopes that the stock will rebound, strategic selling can actually enhance overall portfolio performance.

The other half of this equation, selling as a stock gains in price, should be easier. There's no money to lose in doing that, just the cost of a missed opportunity. That's all right, within reason. But, at the end of the year, you are going to have a portfolio full of winners and losers, and the winners have to outpace the losers. So don't get jumpy about selling into strength. Also, keep in mind that taxes eat into returns. Short-term capital gains rates are taxed as income, as high as 35 percent. Long-term rates, for stocks held 18 months or longer, are now just 15 percent. The government rewards patience on the upside.

Chartists tend to be short-term investors. The technique is mostly popular with day traders, who are trying to make pennies on every trade while limiting losses. But only professional, salaried traders at legitimate firms should have any interest in investing that way. And the best among them also use more than charts as they plan their trading course.

Avoid All Penny Stocks

The Wilshire 5000 contains a lot of names you have never heard of and never will hear of, unless you go looking for them. That total-market index is full of stocks that are so small, and so infrequently traded, that they never ease into the consciousness of most investors. These stocks trade for pocket change and sometimes go weeks or months without trading hands. They are often closely held by founders or company insiders and are, for all intents and purposes, private companies in a public form. Obviously, the low level of liquidity makes them subject to rapid price swings, and that volatility attracts market manipulators who are on the prowl. Since these companies are usually desperate for money, they are also not afraid of working with high-pressure stockbrokers and bucket shops in order to get their shares sold. That's why individual investors should avoid these stocks.

Of course, not all penny stocks engage in or are the result of untoward behavior. Sometimes entrepreneurs who have found themselves turned down by venture capital and private equity funds will merge with a defunct company that still has public status in what's called a reverse merger. That maneuver allows the company to become public without an initial public offering underwritten by an investment bank. This company already has two strikes against it in that it failed to raise private equity funds and then failed to find a bank that would bring it public. But those sins don't seem so unforgivable in light of the tepid venture capital and public offering market in the United States since 2000. One legitimate reason for engineering a reverse merger is that there are hedge funds out there that will buy large chunks of small public companies and then try to help manage those ventures to make them successful. It's like making a venture capital investment in a public company. And there are money managers out there who specialize in such turnaround situations. These companies make great targets, because even a small hedge fund with $10 million could afford to buy some board seats.

That's not a game most individual investors will care to play. Buying a stock because you believe in a company's long-term prospect is one thing, joining the board of directors of a company with three employees head-quartered somewhere in the Dakota badlands is quite another.

A lot of these stocks are sold, over the phone, by brokerage houses that you have never heard of. In most cases, the company can't sell its shares to you directly and has to go through a registered third-party broker. But just because a broker is registered doesn't mean it is one with which you should be doing business. I hate to impugn all upstart brokerages here, but anyone making a cold call about an investment opportunity is not to be trusted. Often, these brokerages have names that are meant to sound like the names of major Wall Street institutions, with words like *Berkshire* and *Morgan* used to invoke some nonexistent and never explicitly addressed in conversation association with Berkshire Hathaway, Morgan Stanley, and the like.

Some readers might be confused about a book that argues in one chapter for the merits of deep value investing and in another warns against the perils of penny stocks. But it's very rare that a penny stock represents shares of a down-on-its-luck, legitimately offered company. Most penny stocks started out below $10 a share. Major corporations that aren't going out of business will usually engineer a reverse split of their shares to keep from being delisted by the major stock markets. When a company doesn't take that face-saving step (like Enron, which now trades for pennies), then it is probably planning its death.

There is a fine line between death and deep value, but if you stick to listed stocks, or companies with market caps greater than $100 million, you won't often have to worry about it.

Don't Short Small Stocks

Forbes magazine runs a page of stock picks in every issue called "Makers and Breakers," and the feature always includes one recommendation for short sellers. But one hard rule that the magazine follows is that it will never recommend that the individual investor short a stock with a market cap below $400 million. In the short sale, liquidity is of paramount importance. That means that the short seller needs to be able to buy back her borrowed shares at a moment's notice. The bane of every short seller is a phenomenon known as the short squeeze that can turn a winning trade into a loser in less than a day.

The short squeeze occurs when too many short sellers try to cover at once. These naysayers are suddenly buying shares on the open market, and that drives the price of the stock up.

One technique for avoiding this situation is to short alone by not shorting stocks that other people are betting against. If there are no other shorts, there is no short squeeze. But other short sellers aren't always the cause of a squeeze. Sometimes, large investors who notice intense short activity around a company will make market-moving investments in the stock, knowing that the short sellers will scramble to limit their losses and that the stock price will receive a short-term boost. Other times, a hapless company will surprise Wall Street with a positive earnings release or even successful test data on a new product that will bring new investors into the stock, causing a surge and short squeeze.

So avoiding other short sellers isn't a foolproof way of avoiding the squeeze. Besides, to short a stock alone implies you have some insight that the rest of the market has somehow missed. It's possible, but you'd better be sure that you do.

The alternative method is to short reasonably large stocks, where there is always stock available for sale. Since volume changes day to day, market cap is a good indicator. Say you're shorting IBM; there's no way that a large investor can cause a short squeeze there. IBM is larger than a lot of mutual funds and hedge funds. A positive earnings announcement might well kill your short position, but it won't result in a squeeze, no matter what's happening to IBM's stock on a given day, it's always being bought and sold by Wall Street specialists.

What short sellers often forget is that company management hates them. For a long time, shorting was considered dirty dealing, an almost unpatriotic act. It is a bit ugly, because it's a bet on failure. IBM doesn't care if you short them because the company's stock is mostly immune to such sentiments from individual investors. But smaller public companies, those with stocks trading over the counter that tend to be tightly held by founders and insiders, do care. Their stocks are illiquid, and some of those companies, even those with market caps approaching $100 million, go weeks without a share of stock changing hands. In this case, the majority owners are in a unique position to punish people with short positions. Sure, it's market manipulation of a sort, but they can't be forced to sell you shares just because you want to buy them.

Aside from the world of mergers and acquisitions, where most of us will never visit, there's nothing more personal than the battle between short sellers and the management team of a small, public company. In this age of faceless, electronic trading, it seems out of place, but there is potential for conflict.

Remember: Being paranoid doesn't necessarily mean they're not out to get you.

Avoid the penny stocks when shorting, and enjoy the anonymity and ease of betting against the giants.

Use a Stop-Loss When Shorting a Stock

"Selling a stock short" is a bet that a security is going to go down in price over a given period of time. Basically, a short seller borrows stock from a brokerage house and sells it. The money from the sale is put into a cash account. Then, the investor waits for the stock's price to drop and buys back the stock, returning it to the lender in what's called "covering the trade." The difference between the sale and purchase price of the stock goes to the investor, while the brokerage house gets its stock back and a trading fee. In principle, the short sale is one of the riskiest trades an investor can make.

Consider this: If you buy stock in ABC Corporation for $50 and the company goes bankrupt and pays nothing to the stockholders, you lose $50. It's a blow, but a finite blow. If you short ABC at $50 and the stock climbs to $100, you also lose $50. But if the stock climbs to $150, you lose $100. Structurally, losses on shorting a stock can be infinite.

It's unlikely that a short play will get so out of hand. But there is that ever-present desire to be right that sometimes makes investors endure losses needlessly. Also, because losses are paper losses, until they are realized when the investor closes his transaction, there's a tendency to wait and be proven correct by history.

One way to prevent this is to set a personal "stop-loss" and stick to it. A stop-loss is just what it sounds like—a preset figure for every transaction that says how much the investor can afford to lose. The figure could be plucked out of the air. (Some people are comfortable losing 10 percent on a trade, others only 3 percent.) Or it could be chosen more scientifically, by examining the performance of each security in a portfolio over a given period of time to figure out what the average winning transaction gains and what the average loser sheds. Since the ultimate goal is for the entire portfolio to be worth more at the end of the year than at the beginning, it would be smart to set the stop-loss so that losses are never larger than wins in percentage terms.

In certain circumstances, the long-only investor has the luxury of time. If a long position isn't leveraged and isn't a major part of an investor's portfolio, then that investor can wait for a price recovery, so long as bankruptcy isn't looming.

The short seller is playing with borrowed securities and the broker has the right to ask for its stock back at prevailing market prices. A short position gone wrong can very quickly eat into other aspects of an investor's portfolio, if extra money is needed to cover the amount.

Along the lines of infinite losses, there's no set standard for how long an investor can keep a short position open. This usually isn't a problem, but it can be. Technically, the broker can call back its shares at any given time. This situation is rare, as the broker has no interest in causing its clients to lose money, but it can occur. If the brokerage house feels it needs its stock back, all it has to do is demand it, and it doesn't matter if the broker's call fits in with the investor's plans.

Usually, short positions aren't held for a long time. Indeed, holding a position for a couple of months makes most short sellers long-term investors. Usually, positions are opened and covered over the course of days or a trading week. So again, the long-only investor has a different mindset that goes along with the different time horizon. If you buy a stock and plan to hold it for more than a year, the fact that it has declined in price during the first month isn't necessarily important. The short seller should know quickly whether he made a good or a bad bet. That's why the stop-loss is so useful: Once the stop-loss is hit, the transaction is ended and there's no reason to wonder about what might have been. On to the next trade!

3

The Federal Reserve

MORE SO THAN the entrepreneurs that made the Internet into the fun and useful place that it's become, Federal Reserve Board Chairman Alan Greenspan might well be *the* financial celebrity of the 1990s. The Federal Reserve, charged with keeping America's banking industry running and keeping money flowing at reasonable levels, is the source of a lot of interest from news watchers and investors alike. Being a collection of mostly men who meet behind closed doors deciding the financial fate of the country, the Fed has its followers among conspiracy buffs as well.

The Fed meets once every six weeks to set its policy on interest rates, and that decision is always a major news event. It keeps pundits busy, first trying to figure out what the Fed will do and then trying to figure out how what they have done will affect the market. Naturally, a few oft-repeated truisms have risen from all this speculation, and that's what we will be examining here.

Don't Fight the Fed

The Federal Reserve holds a special place in the minds of investors, as it seems to manipulate and even control the market through its ability to set interest rates. Whenever the Fed meets, it's a news event, and one topic of interest is always "how will the market react?" The Fed is often spoken of as a "driving force behind the market." Who wants to stand in the way of a quasi-governmental organization that oversees all of the American banking industry?

But the Federal Reserve doesn't exist to regulate or even monitor the stock market. Federal Reserve Board Chairman Alan Greenspan has been most famously concerned with managing inflation by regulating the flow of money through banks in the U.S. system. Of course, this regulation has a great effect on the stock market. But to the Federal Reserve, the stock market is just one indicator that tells board members how the overall economy is doing. It's an important indicator, and one that must be watched, but high or low stock market returns are not ends sought by the Fed. Stock market investors can't ignore the Fed any more than the Fed can ignore the stock market. But Fed interest rate manipulations are a lousy sole basis for making investment decisions.

The Fed's effect on the stock market, simply put, lies in its control over short-term interest rates. When the Fed raises rates, thus tightening the flow of dollars, companies have a harder time raising debt or equity in order to expand. That means that growth rates falter and stock prices fall. When the Fed loosens the money supply, companies have an easier time expanding and the stock market grows with them.

But it's impossible to say when, exactly, the markets will react to Fed decisions. Greenspan noticed that the economy's quick growth during the late 1990s, expressed in part by the rise of the Nasdaq to over 5000 and the Dow to 12,000, was not sustainable. He chided investors for succumbing to "irrational exuberance," and over time he raised interest rates to 6.25 percent in an effort to slow things down. The market didn't crash until March of 2000. In that case, fighting the Fed worked for a long time.

The same thing happened after the market fell. Since March of 2000 the Federal Reserve has eased interest rates nine times to a historic low of just 1.25 percent. But corporate America didn't immediately respond to the offer of available money, and investors, still licking their wounds from the spring of 2000, didn't jump back into the market. Not even the Fed can force people to buy things they feel they don't need.

In July of 2002, Andrew Smithers wrote in London's *Evening Standard* that the Fed might have run out of ammunition when the stock market dropped a third of its value in the face of its rate cuts. "The Fed is probably scared that if it cuts rates again when they are already so low, this will be seen as a sign of panic."

If "don't fight the Fed" had held true, then the market shouldn't have been tanking in the face of massive interest rate reductions. One possibility for the Fed's failure is that other events outside the Fed's control had served to depress the market. First, there was a wave of corporate scandal that is still winding its way through the courts. Investors had lost faith in stock analysts, stockbrokers, and investment banks that were all shown to have interests in conflict with their retail clients. Investors were burned in corporate boardrooms as Enron, WorldCom, Tyco, Qwest, and HealthSouth were all hurt or debilitated by scandals ranging from alleged shady accounting to CEOs who allegedly dodged sales taxes while amassing high-end art collections. Even the great Jack Welch, the retired chief executive of General Electric, who some had revered as an almost godlike manager, became the target of ire for his generous retirement compensation. The September 11 terrorist attacks in the United States, the subsequent war in Afghanistan, and a war in Iraq a year later also served to stymie the stock market. Interest rates are no doubt important, but they are hardly the most important news of the day.

Economists often describe Fed rate cuts as having a lagging effect on the economy. But there is no good consensus of opinion as to when the economy and the stock market will register the joy or pain of an interest rate change. Some say it happens in three months, others say nine months or a year. There's no point in investing on that uncertainty.

Trust in the Greenspan Put

Even while Federal Reserve Board Chairman Alan Greenspan chided investors for their irrational exuberance, many investors were talking about the "Greenspan put." It meant that Alan Greenspan loved the stock market, realized that its continued rise was necessary for the long-term health of the U.S. economy, and would never let it fall. Boy, were they ever wrong!

The Federal Reserve doesn't care about the stock market. The job of the Fed is to regulate the nation's money supply, keep inflation under control, and try to manage the economy toward full employment for all Americans. Major stock market advances are arguably at odds with the Fed's inflation-fighting mission.

Remember that in the late 1990s, for example, real estate prices in the technology capital of California's Bay Area skyrocketed. Rents and purchasing prices were out of control. The same thing happened in New York City, Boston, and Washington, D.C., where Americans flocked to find work in the new technology industry. All of these new people, spending as if their paper worth were real, drove prices up. Sure, productivity gains kept inflation under control, which allowed companies to raise prices only slightly but to make more money on better margins. But without those productivity gains, the bubble would have burst much sooner than it did, because the Fed would have had to act even more harshly to combat inflation.

While folks were talking about the Greenspan put, and loving Greenspan as the maestro behind the markets, Greenspan was actually publicly working to take them down. He raised interest rates between 1998 and 2000. He didn't begin to cut rates until after the market crash in 2000.

Still, major firms like Merrill Lynch and bond-market investment god Bill Gross of PIMCO spoke openly about the belief that Greenspan would limit the amount to which stock prices could fall. It was thought

Greenspan would expand the money supply whenever there was any sustained, downward movement in the markets.

On April 14, 2000, Greenspan actually dispelled the notion that he had any such intentions, warning investors that the Fed would only intervene in the event of a major market calamity and would not hold the market's hand on the road to high returns.

Two Tumbles and a Jump

The immediate market impact of decisions made by the Federal Reserve tends to fade quickly. Nevertheless, the Fed does have an undeniable long-term effect on the economy and thus the market. The maxim "two tumbles and a jump" says that any time the Federal Reserve lowers interest rates twice in a row, the market is in for a rollicking good ride. Since the Fed only meets every six weeks, the two tumbles have to occur within a three-month period, so don't watch for big daily moves. The jump in two tumbles and a jump might occur immediately, or it might occur months after the tumbles as the effect of the interest rate cuts wind their way through the economy.

Norman Fosback developed two tumbles and a jump for the Institute of Econometric Research back in 1972. The principle actually covers more than just interest rates, predicting that the market will rise if the Fed lowers short-term rates, the banking reserve requirement, or the margin requirement twice in a row. Twenty days after the Fed acts twice, the S&P 500 is usually up 4 percent. After three months, the index is up 11 percent, and it's up nearly 30 percent if you can wait a year.

In 1998, *BusinessWeek* ran an article headlined "The Case for the Dow 10,000," in the midst of a 1700 point Dow rally over two months. The author of the article, Jeffrey Laderman, cited two tumbles and jump as one reason that the stock market was able to rebound after the Asian currency crises and related debt crisis in Latin America.

When the Fed cuts interest rates, it becomes cheaper to borrow money. Consumers can refinance their mortgages, thus lowering their monthly payments and freeing up cash that can be either spent or invested. Recent rate cuts allowed automakers to boost their sales by offering 0 percent financing on car loans. The Fed's rate cuts in the face of the 2001 recession certainly helped take the hurt out of hard economic times and enabled consumer confidence to remain high where it might have otherwise plummeted. But the unemployment rate still climbed and businesses still didn't expand at the rate investors had become accustomed to. Faced with the prospect of easy money, corporations went about refinancing and paying off their own debts. Going forward, that's good for the market because it means that corporate America's balance sheets will be stronger. But it had little positive short-term impact on investment portfolios.

Economists differ about how long it takes for a single Federal Reserve action to have an effect on the economy. Most put the time frame at between six to nine months. The stock market, which is placing bets on the economy's future might react a little more quickly. But remember that a prolonged bear market can certainly endure interest rate cuts. Between 2000 and the end of 2002, the Federal Reserve dropped interest rates from 6.25 percent in January of 2001 to 1.25 percent by the end of 2002. A recovery in the stock market didn't begin to take hold until the latter part of 2003.

Interest rate cuts undoubtedly stimulate the economy. But the Fed makes no promises to investors about when that stimulus will be realized in the price of their stocks.

It used to be true, by the way, that interest rate cuts were terrible for bank stocks because cutting the price at which banks can lend money cuts right into core earnings. These days, after years of consolidation in the banking sector, most banks call themselves "financial services companies" and draw their revenues from a variety of sources. Well-diversified banks can now weather falling interest rates quite well and need not necessarily be avoided when the Fed cuts rates.

Three Steps and a Stumble

Walking hand in hand with two tumbles and a jump is "three steps and a stumble," which says that if the Fed raises interest rates three times in a row, the stock market will fall. It is true that cutting interest rates has a stimulative effect on the economy and that raising rates is one of the tools that the Fed uses to cool down an economy that's growing too fast. Since the stock market thrives on a fast-growing economy, investors aren't bound to be happy to hear that things are going to slow down.

The Federal Reserve raised interest rates for the third time in a row in February of 2000, and the market slid a month later, recovered a bit, and then closed down for the year, with the S&P 500 shedding 10 percent of its value.

But rising rates aren't always a sign that the economy is going to be terrible in the future. The Fed wants to engineer sustainable growth, not to cause a disaster.

Moderate rises in interest rates are a natural part of a booming economy. Think of it this way: As the economy grows, so does the demand for money. The simple notion of supply and demand says that if demand is hot and supply is constant, prices are going up. A healthy economy should show some moderate uptick in the demand for money. Of course, if money becomes too expensive to borrow, consumers will lay low and companies will put off plans for expansion. That results in the kind of economic slowdown that is partially expressed in poor stock market returns.

The effects of both interest rate hikes and cuts are difficult to determine in advance. Though it is generally true that higher rates depress the economy and lower rates egg it on, there is no set schedule for when the stock market will react to either. The Federal Reserve started raising rates in 1999, and the S&P 500 turned in a 21 percent return.

Investors didn't need to watch the Fed to see that Internet, technology, and telecommunications stocks had gone quickly through the roof and that they might not land softly. Though it's tempting to blame Alan Greenspan for quashing the bull market, he had no reason for doing so. What really killed the technology run was an endemic part of the technology cycle: When new servers, processors, and fiber optics are introduced to the market, companies can charge a premium. Once competitors get in on the act, prices fall dramatically. Demand also slackens as businesses and consumers realize they have enough computing power at their disposal (at least for now) in order to meet daily needs. Demand for underground fiber also slackened, and billions borrowed in order to build new communications networks went unpaid when customers couldn't be found to populate the lines.

The Federal Reserve might have stymied some company's plans to lease fiber-optic space, but I doubt it. It seems as if corporate America already had all the fiber it wanted. Whether money is cheap or expensive doesn't matter when folks don't need to borrow.

The fact is that an entire sector of companies temporarily lost pricing power during 2000, and a bear market resulted. The Fed might have hastened those circumstances, but it didn't cause them. For investors, following market fundamentals is as good as following the Fed any day.

4

The Smart
Money Talks

STOCK ANALYSTS, brokers, fund managers, corporate insiders, and, yes, financial writers all claim the "smart money" mantle. Investors, faced with making decisions that will affect themselves and perhaps generations of family members, would all like to meet a perfect guru who can walk them through the complicated world of financial planning. Many of those christened with the Smart Money moniker are, of course, those who utter the truisms dealt with throughout this book. They have also come up with a few that tell you to keep listening to them.

Actively Managed Funds Outperform in Down Markets

When the market is down and folks want answers, they are willing to believe that a smart-money manager is worth her or his fee. Active fund managers are believed to be able to beat indexes in down markets because they can jump out of the market altogether, holding funds in cash reserves while a fund wedded to the S&P 500 will have to follow the index for richer or poorer. Active managers can also avoid large-cap stocks that are in decline. Because the S&P 500 weights itself by company market caps, a giant like 3M or Ford will have a larger effect on the index's performance than a small-cap company. Active managers can dump Ford early, while the index has to own it in proportion to its size.

The Schwab Center for Investment Research has managed to debunk this myth, pointing out that active managers have trailed index funds in 55 percent of down markets, despite their freedom from the tyranny of index cohesion.

Schwab examined 20 down-market periods between one and seven months long, starting in September 1987 and ending in March 2001. The index funds won out 11 times, which is basically a tie. During the longest down market, between September 2000 and March 2001, the index funds lost 23.25 percent and the actively managed funds lost 23.29 percent. Again, managed funds and index funds are basically tied.

But, if the freedom of active management is the key to beating a bear market, so the theory goes, then the longer the market is in decline, the better life should get for fund managers. After all, money market accounts don't lose money and fixed-income securities are often quite attractive for stocks during bear markets. The problem is that fund managers are paid stock pickers. They will have a lot to answer for if they park enormous sums of their assets under management in cash accounts. There's no point to investors paying 1.4 percent a year to have a manager put their money in the bank for them, and the managers know that.

Most large, actively managed funds also can't avoid the blue chips that are dragging down the indexes. Mutual funds are prohibited from placing more than 5 percent of their assets in any one security, and they are prohibited from owning more than 10 percent of any company. A fund with billions under management that wants to remain fully invested in the stock market will never find enough liquid stocks for its portfolio if the manager ignores the top 30 in the S&P 500.

Schwab did find one thing: In the instances where active managers were right, they were really right. When the managers beat the indexes, they did so by 1.64 percent on average, while when the indexes won, they did so by only 0.58 percent. But again, the data is warped a bit by the type of markets we are talking about. During modest declines of up to 5 percent, the actively managed funds won seven of their nine victories over the indexers. When the market fell more than 5 percent, the index funds won six times and the active managers only won twice. So it seems that active managers can stave off losses in the short term but they tend to experience the pain of the indexes as time wears on.

Consider also that an index is an index. All an investor needs to do is find one with the lowest fees and the greatest tax efficiency, and those are usually Vanguard products. But all actively managed funds are different. There's a lot of subjective decision making when one shops for an active mutual fund, and the hardest question to answer is whether a manager is worth his fee. Other chapters in this book show that there is nothing wrong with actively managed funds and that some of them really do outperform over the long haul. But Schwab has proven that it doesn't make sense to jump in and out of managed funds to chase outperformance in down markets. Besides, down markets are tricky because it's hard to predict when they will start or how long they will last.

If you're an indexer, stay an indexer. If you want to hire a manager, hire a manager, but don't worry about up and down markets when it comes to making that decision.

Follow the Fund Managers

Since the Securities and Exchange Commission put regulatory filings online, even investors with the slowest of dial-up Internet connections can see the major holdings of their favorite mutual fund managers on a quarterly basis. But a quarter behind is too far behind for investors planning to mirror the actions of their favorite manager. Obviously, mutual funds want to sell their service, and there's no way that the powerful industry lobby, the Investment Company Institute, is going to allow for any more transparency when it comes to a manager's holdings. Still, there are good ideas to be gleaned from these filings and from comments that managers make in the press.

One thing that a mutual fund's holdings report can offer is evidence of long-term favorites. Some managers will hold on to favorite stocks for years, constantly adding to their positions. The filings will show, on a quarterly basis, what positions were increased or decreased over those months. It won't say what prices the manager paid, but tracking this information is a good way to find solid companies that the pros believe in. But do be careful about price. Mutual funds have access to shares of new issues, usually right at or even below the announced market price. A good buy for them could be a ripoff by the time it's available to you. The mutual fund filings won't ever tell you exactly what to buy, but they can provide inspiration for your own stock research.

A weakness to this approach is that you know nothing about motivation, and a fund manager has different goals than the average investor. For one thing, managers are paid to keep money actively in the markets and so they are loath to go to cash for fear that investors will feel gypped paying 1.4 percent of assets for a bank account.

Managers also have to meet redemptions when investors decide to leave the market. Sometimes, if there's not enough new money coming in to cover the old money leaving, managers have to liquidate positions in order to pay the departing investors. Such moves tell little about the managers' feelings about a certain stock.

Another tactic would be to examine the holdings of a favorite fund from a fundamental point of view. The mutual fund reporting service Morningstar will tell you the average price-to-earnings multiple of a given portfolio. Such information could be a good standard of fair value when you are building your own portfolio. You can also find out the average market cap of a stock in a fund's portfolio. If your favorite manager likes mid-cap stocks, you might want to check out that sector.

Some managers refuse to make specific stock recommendations in the financial press, while others are happy to tout their picks. Most television networks like CNBC, CNN, and CNNfn require managers to disclose whether or not they own a stock that they are discussing on television. It's not uncommon for managers to give more information and say that they are buying a stock. They are less likely to say what they are selling, because such comments can be construed as a criticism of the company. Liability demands that commentators tread carefully into that territory.

Like investment banks, and every other part of the financial services industry, mutual funds and their managers do run into frequent conflicts of interest. Chances are that your company's 401(k) plan is administered by one of the major fund families in the United States. If you work for a major public corporation, the fund family that runs the 401(k) plan might well own stock in the company too. A manager from that fund family will probably not say anything that would jeopardize the 401(k) business, so overt, critical comments would be unlikely. You never can tell.

Remember also that mutual funds will often invest in securities that might not be right for the average investor. Some mutual funds are allowed to short stock, or to be against the market with put options. Even the vanilla [S&P] 500 Index Fund by Vanguard uses S&P futures in order to generate a return that actually beats the index it tracks. A mutual fund might also trade its holdings more feverishly than would be advisable for an individual. Since the mutual fund's asset bases are so much higher than an individual's, it pays less to trade stocks. Even so, trading costs do diminish mutual fund returns, so imagine the effect on a smaller, individual portfolio, where the investor is paying between $10 and $30 a trade.

It would be a waste, of course, to completely ignore the actions of some of the best money managers in the business. Just don't try to copy them. The game's just not set up that way.

The Longer That Institutional Investors Hold a Stock, the Less Volatile It Will Be

Some investors believe that institutions like banks, mutual funds, hedge funds, and big pension funds can help cut down on a stock's volatility because these large investors are sluggish in their trades. There is also a sense that institutions are the true market movers and that since volatility isn't in their interests, their favorite stocks will remain less volatile. The problem is that institutions are powerful but not all-powerful. A 1999 paper by Burton G. Malkiel of the Princeton University Economics Department shows that, at the turn of the century, individual stock volatility was up across the board while the volatility of the market at large remained stable throughout the twentieth century. Malkiel calls individual stock volatility "idiosyncratic." If the institutional theory is right, this idiosyncratic volatility shouldn't be showing up.

First, we have to look at the market as it is today. Since the late 1970s, and especially in the 1980s, the mutual fund industry has grown astronomically. There were about 300 domestic equity funds around during the late 1970s. There were so few that when *Forbes* magazine published its annual fund survey, it printed performance results for every fund on the market. These days, with more than 5000 funds operating, managers have to jump through hoops to make the magazine's cut.

The largest 100 financial institutions in the United States own 50 percent of the stocks traded in the country. Though mutual funds aren't allowed to own more than 5 percent of a company's stock, mutual fund families, big companies like Fidelity and T. Rowe Price, can own large blocks of corporate stock. Fidelity has $330 billion invested in the stock market, and it owns 20 percent of Pathmark Stores and 18 percent of Playboy Enterprises. Janus Capital Management, adviser to the Janus mutual funds, owns 10 percent of Apria Healthcare. The Vanguard Fund Group owns 13 percent of Readers Digest and 5 percent of Comcast.

These positions can't be dumped quickly, because it would depress the stock price on the way down, causing losses for all of the funds. The managers in one fund family can't all act in concert to liquidate a position. A quick dumping of stock by every fund manager in a single family would surely draw the ire of regulatory authorities, who would accuse the funds of market manipulation if they were to try to do so.

Examining the market for volatility between 1926 and 1997, Malkiel found no discernible trends of upward volatility in the overall market. There were spikes, of course, around the late 1920s and the 1930s as the Great Depression took hold, and there were spikes in the 1970s during the energy crisis. The market crash of 1987 was also a time of high volatility. But overall, trends aren't discernible.

When Malkiel turned to the issue of individual stocks, however, he started to find that volatility increases. "On any specific day, the most volatile individual stocks move by extremely large percentages. It is not uncommon on a single trading day to find that several stocks have changed in price by 25 percent or more. Indeed, price changes of over 50 percent in a single day for some stocks (excluding new issues) are not at all uncommon."

The institutions are at least partly to blame, says Malkiel. He writes that institutions have increased their share of the market sevenfold since 1950 and that block trades of over 10,000 shares now account for half of the market's daily volume. Malkiel's data says that individual stocks are more volatile when they are largely owned by institutions because these big investors, who change their minds about stocks and the markets as frequently as retail investors do, can more quickly and decisively act on new information about individual stocks.

Never mind that these institutions probably get the information first. Even if you and a Fidelity fund manager got a piece of information about a stock at the same time, you would have to spend the day figuring out what the information means. The fund manager, on the other hand, can call a meeting of his analysts, who will have an answer before you are done searching the Yahoo! Finance message boards. Also, what Fidelity decides will have much greater bearing on the stock price than what you decide.

Remember also that while you can figure out what institutions own what percentage of what stocks (this data will often be in a company's proxy or annual report), you will likely never know why they own it. A fund company's ownership might reflect decisions of a bear market fund manager in a bull market. Or it might simply express the bias of certain fund families that concentrate on technology or growth stocks. Banks often own stocks for their trading accounts or on behalf of their brokerage clients.

When it comes to the larger stocks, some pension funds, banks, and mutual funds will have no choice but to own large chunks, for diversification purposes. Their interests are not your interests. Unless you know why another investor or institution owns a stock, you don't really know much. So it's best to leave the laborious work of trying to figure out who knows what to the side so you can get on with the laborious work of figuring out which stocks are fairly priced and which aren't.

Pay Attention to an Analyst's Price Targets

When issuing a report on a company, a stock analyst usually includes a price target. It's meant to say, in part, that the analysis applies to the company until it reaches a certain price, in which case, the analyst might change the recommendation based on valuation. It makes a certain amount of sense, because a stock that's a bargain at $20 a share might not be worth buying at $35. Unfortunately, what many analysts mean by price target is that they expect the stock to grow to at least that level. Investors pick up on this by thinking that they are buying a stock that will almost surely rise to the level of its target. That's a mistake.

Wall Street analysts are easy to pick on these days, but for a few years their price targets were taken as gospel. The problem with this veneration is that analyst's targets are often arbitrary; they are the last things done before an analyst's report is vetted by lawyers and sent to the investing public.

It was, after all, Henry Blodget (then at Merrill Lynch) who told me a few months after the technology crash that he was getting out of issuing price targets altogether. "I'm getting away from price targets because they distract from the fundamental work we've been doing," he said. "You have to question the validity of putting a pinpoint price target on any equity security."

Around the same time, I spoke with Gary Helmig, an analyst at the tech-oriented investment bank Wit SoundView, who said that "we do them [price targets] because the sales force likes to have it to talk about." Price targets were, are, and always will be marketing tools. Despite all the talk about independent research, remember that analysts are separated only from the investment banking side of the business—those folks who ink multimillion-dollar mergers and equity financings. They aren't separated from the retail brokers who work the phones to sell stocks to individual investors. Analysts are salespeople who just don't necessarily work on commission.

Analysts who actually do think that a company is well managed and has good long-term prospects are often forced to add an optimistic price target to their report. They do so in order to justify giving the company a positive recommendation. At some firms, the analysts' handbook will actually say that a "strong buy" rating means that the analyst expects a 25 percent appreciation in the stock price over the next year. That means that an analyst has to add 25 percent to the price to give it the best recommendation. The target becomes an almost arbitrary appendage to the rest of the report. Most analysts spend a lot more time examining a company's financials and talking with suppliers, customers, and insiders than they do in conjuring their price target numbers. That's as it should be.

It's best, when presented with an analyst's report, to cover up both the recommendation and the price target and to read the report and come to your own conclusion. Never expect that a stock will reach or surpass its target. Buy it at a fair value and sell it if the value is diminished. That target is a number that you can't count on.

Follow the Smart Money

We all tend to believe that somebody has the answers. There are, after all, gargantuan salaries paid all throughout the financial services industry, and to earn such tidy keeps, there must be some special talents out there. But who is the smart money? The definition changes from day to day, it seems. During the Internet boom, analysts like Henry Blodget, Mary Meeker, and Jack Grubman were considered to be the smart money. When Henry Blodget predicted that Amazon.com shares would climb to above $300, investors piled on to make his prediction into reality. In fact, they made his prediction seem conservative by trading the shares up to $600. For a time, those analysts were the smart money. After the crash, investors made a hobby out of suing the smart money to reclaim what they had lost while acting as members of a woolly investing flock.

Christopher Johnson, the director of quantitative analysis for Schaffer's Investment Research, believes that following analysts is a sure-fire way to be late in purchasing the best stocks. "If 25 analysts cover a stock and 24 have a buy rating on it, then there's no more money going in," he says. "By that point, anyone who wants to own the stock has already bought shares and it's not going up."

According to Johnson, the analysts that represent smart money often cause an initial buzz about a stock that they are recommending or opining that investors need to take a position in. This buzz causes an increase in the sideline money that becomes allocated to a stock, and this event happens quickly. The problem is that this sideline money is a finite resource, and once investors have allocated their money to the "hot stock," there is no longer money to buy the stock to move the price higher. Additionally, the fact that investors are "all in" on the hot stock adds nervousness to the price, as there is now an extremely large amount of potential selling pressure in the stock. So the slightest bad news can cause these stocks to sell off dramatically. Quips Johnson: "Normally we hear terms like 'irrational selling' when this is occurring."

One place that Johnson looks for stocks is in the pile of companies that analysts either dislike or ignore completely. He wants to find stocks before they are deemed worthy of coverage by the big banks.

Johnson also takes another smart-money set to task, believing that major cover stories on companies by business magazines seem to cause a curse. Actually, he doesn't believe in magic: Instead, he thinks that by the time a company rises to the level where a magazine will try to use it to sell newsstand copies, it's likely too well known to be anything but overbought. "Unless the company not only lives up to but exceeds those expectations set in the article, individuals get nervous and they normally begin to sell," says Johnson.

Company insiders are often labeled "smart money," and it is sometimes fun to watch them buy and sell stock in the companies with which they are so intimately involved. But it's not clear that watching their trades is a great way to get consistently good information. Call investor relations at any company where a board member or the CEO has announced an intention to sell a large chunk of stock; you will be assured that the insider is selling for the purposes of diversifying his or her personal portfolio. It's a stock answer, just like companies will say that a high-level executive is leaving to "pursue other interests" rather than "can't get along with a single colleague in the building." The thing is, the stock answer is often true.

The JPMorgan Private Bank specializes in managing the money of high-net-worth folks who are often company insiders. The fact that these smart-money people often hire bankers to handle their accounts is proof enough that the smart money isn't so smart that it doesn't want advice. One of the first things a JPMorgan banker has to do when she has a company insider for a client is to force him to diversify. An entrepreneur that became wealthy by founding a company is often loath to sell that company's stock, because it has worked well for him so far. But the very rich need to diversify if they want to remain rich. So they will invariably have to sell stock in the companies they run. And those stock sales really don't say much about the actual prospects of the company.

Remember that insiders haven't, for the most part, bought their stock on the open market. They have been inside for a long time and probably might even have enjoyed options that have allowed them to buy stock at a discount to prevailing market prices. If you have gotten into a company at $10 a share and the CEO paid $1 for his shares, then the boss can sell as you buy and pocket a huge return while you will have to wait. You will also often find company insiders buying while the share price is dropping. Maybe that event signals that the insider thinks his stock is a good buy and he's bargain hunting. But it might also be a public relations move. There's no way of getting inside the smart money's head.

Sometimes insiders are just plain wrong about the future of their company stock. ImClone founder Sam Waksal was convicted of insider trading after dumping shares in the company he founded on a tip that the company's cancer drug, Erbitux, wasn't going to be approved by the U.S. Food and Drug Administration. About a year-and-a-half later, as Waksal was sentenced to 87 months in prison and to pay $8 million in fines, European researchers reported that Erbitux was extending the lives of gravely ill colon cancer patients. Had Waksal stuck by his company he not only would have avoided prison but possibly could have enjoyed an ImClone renaissance.

The final members of the smart-money class are the money managers at mutual funds and hedge funds. The problem is that mutual funds file holdings reports quarterly. So if you want to mimic a manager, you will be three months behind the manager's trades. Hedge funds don't file their holdings at all. And there have been examples (most recently, Gotham Capital Partners) of hedge funds that will broadcast their desires to buy and sell in the hopes that investors will pile in or out of a stock. The funds, of course, profit from the trading volume they have created.

In the end, investors are alone with their returns, and every individual has her or his own reason for investing. The smart money might really be smart, but if you are going to follow any advice it should be the advice of someone whose interests are aligned with yours. Smart-money brains are used in the service of smart-money interests. Those interests might not coincide with your own.

Economists Can Predict the Future

Economists are held in high esteem by the investing public because they tend to be thoughtful, well-educated thinkers who are more like scientists or scholars than the usual profit-hungry denizens of the financial world. Economists at think tanks, universities, and investment banks have never had the same conflicts of interest that plague stock analysts. When they work for the big banks, their prognostications about interest rates and trade deficits are used either for the bond-trading desk or to give the bank a bit of intellectual prestige. One reason these economists are important to stock investors, though, is that they tend to be Federal Reserve watchers, and the Federal Reserve has an impact on the performance of the stock market.

One problem with watching economists is that you are not necessarily sure what their motives are. Some of them are clearly trying to make predictions, while others are policy wonks, making recommendations. Wayne Angell, chief economist at Bear Stearns, was once a governor of the Federal Reserve and thus knows Alan Greenspan personally. Because of his very public connection to the Maestro, investors and the business media often seek out Angell when the Federal Reserve meets.

But on February 23, 2001, the folly of this endeavor was revealed. Angell publicly proclaimed that the Federal Reserve would meet to cut interest rates in advance of its scheduled meeting for March 20. Angell's followers listened and bought into the stock market, in anticipation of the short-term jump in equity prices that might accompany such a move. The Dow was down as far as 232 points on February 23 and finally finished 88 points behind.

The rate cut had failed to materialize, and a miffed investor upbraided Angell for being too optimistic. Angell replied: "I said, 'When it became evident that the Fed was not going to do what I so strongly said they should do, did you sell stocks?' He said, 'No.' I said, 'Well, I did.'"

Angell's defense here is that he wasn't making a prediction, he was making a recommendation. The Fed should have cut rates, but it failed to do so, and so Angell sold out of the stock market. Perhaps it was just a misunderstanding, but it's something to watch out for if you are investing on the advice of a favorite economist.

Economists don't just follow the Fed for the fun of it. One reason Federal Reserve moves are so important is that they affect long-term bond yields. (The yields are themselves a signal about how bond traders feel about the economy, which thus affects the stock market over the long run.) The bond yield can go up or down, or it can stay the same. So guessing randomly, economists should be right 33 percent of the time. James Bianco, president of Chicago-based Bianco Research, studied their calls since 1982 and found that the economists were only right on the long bond 28 percent of the time.

Economists are also a bit behind the times, though it's their job to be ahead of things. In aggregate, the economists predicted a 30 percent rise in the Nasdaq for 1999. The index actually rose 86 percent. Perhaps realizing they were too conservative about 1999 they called for a 61 percent gain in 2001. But in that year the Nasdaq dropped 40 percent.

This isn't to say that economists aren't incredibly smart, because they are. Economics might be called the "dismal science," but there is no doubt that anyone who really wants to understand society will have to become familiar with economic terms. It's just that economists seem to be better at explaining the past than at predicting the immediate future, and that limitation affects their utility as dispensers of investment advice.

5

It's That Time of Year

INVESTING IN THE MARKET on certain months but not others, or before or after various holidays, is known as "seasonal investing." A lot of old Wall Street saws have it that there are just certain times of the year, or any given month, where it's best to invest or best to go to cash. The problem with all of these theories is that the market would never let a regularly scheduled opportunity for profit go unexploited. Were it true that stocks always went up in September, then you can bet that a firm like Goldman Sachs would buy up the market in August, preset a sale on October 1, and spend all that money throughout the rest of the year. You can also be sure that everyone else in the market would try it too, driving up stocks at the end of August and causing an enormous crash on each and every first trading day of October. So Goldman Sachs, being clever, would start buying in July, anticipating the August rush. It might work once, but everyone else would catch on. Let's face it, if investing were this easy, it would be simply impossible to invest.

The January Effect

The January effect predicts a jump in stock market prices during the first month of the year. In its original form, the myth is backed up by a reasonable assumption: Investors tend to sell losers out of their portfolio in December so that they can be taken as tax losses to offset capital gains throughout the year. The practice depresses the market in December and leaves money on the sidelines that can fuel a January bump. The effect is mostly centered on small-cap companies, probably signaling an investor's willingness to invest in smaller growth stocks that will yield larger gains throughout the year. That, combined with natural optimism at the beginning of the year, should make for a good first month of trading.

The problem is that it should be impossible for a month or season to have a definitive effect on stock prices. If such calendar-based mojo actually worked, after all, then the entire investment community would know about it months in advance and their attempts to make money on those trades would forever alter the calendar landscape.

The Charles Schwab Center for Investment Research has found, when looking at data from January 1926 through December 2002, that both small-cap stocks and large caps have performed well in January. Small caps have jumped an amazing 5.4 percent, on average, in January. Small caps also had good months in July and November, but they jumped just 1.6 percent. So the long-term data supports the January effect for small caps. Large caps actually turn in their best month in July (1.8 percent), with 1.6 percent gains in January and November as the next best months. So for large caps, it seems that the January effect is negligible.

Schwab has tracked the waning power of the January effect over recent history. To focus on the January effect, Schwab broke the market up into groups, arranged by market caps and measured the performance of stocks in each market-cap group against their performance in other months. If the January effect is real and still going strong, there should be major performance deviations across the board. In the period between

1926 and 1976, Schwab found such variation. But those differences have contracted over time.

That contraction makes sense. The longer the January effect exists, the less power it will have. If an investor knows that small-cap stocks will bounce in January, then why not buy them in December when they are oversold? Of course, such buying in December would bolster prices in December, thus leaving less upside for January and diminishing the January effect.

The Schwab study, "Buy in May and Go Away," actually debunks the notion of the January effect a bit: January is the third best performing month since 1926, but it trails December. December should be a seller's month but it isn't. So the December sell-off, the very cause of the January effect, might not even exist.

Between 1990 and 1999, small-cap stocks outperformed large caps in January less than half the time, though small caps still turned in a robust 2.3 percent return, on average. The very fact that small caps don't win out every time, or even most of the time, shows that while the January effect numbers look good over a long period of time, the phenomenon is not without frequent failure. In January 2000, 2001, and 2002, the small caps swept the large caps, but that phenomenon might well comment on the mood of the market. January 2000 was a boom month, with investors willing to take risks on small growth stocks. January 2001 and January 2002 were months of promised recovery where, again, small-cap stocks were popular because they represent the most upside potential should the entire market rise for the year. Perhaps the key to understanding the myth of the January effect isn't to take the wide view but to examine each year on a case-by-case basis. If there's a reason other than the fact that it's January that's bolstering stock prices, then investors can't count on the month to serve the portfolio.

A consistent, foolproof, everybody-make-money month is just never going to happen, because there will always be investors who try to make more money by taking advantage of the rigid schedule it follows. That very act messes up the schedule. Call it Heisenberg's uncertainty principle of investing: You can't get involved without changing the game.

Take Profits on the First Trading Days of the Month

There's something about the start of things that seems to get investor's interest. The January effect says that small-cap stocks will drive the market to higher returns for the first month of the year. This myth says that returns are best in the first week of any month. Of course, if this were true, then everyone would know it. And if everyone knew about it, it would become impossible to make money on the phenomenon.

Let's take a look at the first week of trading throughout 2002. In the first week of trading during each month, the S&P 500 closed up six times and down six times. You can't get less decisive than that in terms of pattern building. What's worse for this myth is that the down weeks were terrible while the good weeks were blasé. In the down weeks, the S&P 500 lost 158 points, with the worst first week coming in March, when the market dropped 58 points. The up weeks offered 81 points to the index.

None of this means that the reverse of the myth is true, that the market will be down after the first trading days of the month. Data can say interesting things. I chose 2002 in order to see if a trend emerged. Had I chosen another year, I might have seen a trend and proclaimed this myth a flawless pearl from the Street. It's all about what data set you are using.

Because we tend to look for hard and true answers in life and investing, we want to believe data when it's presented. Numerical data holds special providence because, as folks are fond of saying, "numbers don't lie." But they do. Data must not only be present in order to verify a trend or myth, it must be reasonable.

Let's pretend that in the last decade, the stock market always went up in the first trading days of every month and that you could always sell your stocks for a gain as soon as they were over. Forget that everyone would be doing it, causing terrible market declines on the first day of the second week of the month. You have to ask, "Why is this happening, and how do I know it will happen again next month?"

The fact that it happened 25 months running says nothing about what will happen on the twenty-sixth month. The sun won't rise in the east tomorrow because it rose in the east yesterday or even because it's done that every day for millions of years. It rises in the east because of the way the Earth spins on its axis. In the absence of some fundamental reason, all data must be questioned, not in terms of its veracity, but in terms of its predictive power.

Most of the myths in this book take the form of "common sense," but it's actually common sense and a little elementary logic that proves them unreliable.

As January Goes, So Goes the Year

January is often known as "the barometer" month because it's believed that the performance of the market in its first month indicates whether the market will be up or down for the year. Since 1950, the S&P has followed the January trend all but 10 times.

But consider this myth in the context of the January effect, which says that the market rallies in January as investors plow money into the small-cap stock sector. If you believe in the January effect, you can't also believe that January is the barometer month, because then the market would never be down for the year. The January effect would start us on a high note, and the January barometer would then report that the year would end positively. Because we know that some years have been rotten for stocks (most recently, 2000, 2001, and 2002), then we know logically that either the January barometer is wrong, the January effect doesn't hold, or that both of them are nonsense.

One problem with this theory, from an investor's standpoint, is that the myth says that January will predict the direction for the year, not for the following 11 months. So if you are waiting for a January indication, with the intention of jumping in or staying out on February 1, beware. In 1987, January indicated an up year for the market, and indeed, the S&P 500 Index climbed 2 percent by the end of December. But, the market had a 13.2 percent gain that year in January alone. If you had waited until the end of January and decided to invest because January had been a good month, you would have finished the year down 10 percent.

Despite the massive failure in 1987, January has been a decent indicator of stock performance in the following 11 months since 1950. It was wrong only 13 times. Probably, the success of the January indicator is the result of coincidence. Before making investment decisions based on this monthly barometer, try to think of a few plausible reasons why January performance should *cause* the rest of the year to follow suit. You should do so because the only thing an investor can depend on, when looking for patterns in the market, is a causal connection between the pattern and the result. Winning at the blackjack gaming tables every Monday for three years is a coincidence—unless the gambler knows that the Monday blackjack dealer is terrible at his job.

One of the pitfalls of myths like this one is that they only gain currency because, over time, a pattern has emerged. Hold out for an explanation of that pattern before making decisions based on it.

The First Week of Trading Determines the Year

While some investors believe that stock market returns for the month of January will determine stock performance for the rest of the year, a less patient set of investors only want to wait a week to know how the year will go. The data behind this particular myth is entirely confusing, and it's a wonder that this notion is repeated so often in investment circles.

Between 1990 and 2002, the first week of the year has predicted the direction of the stock market, as measured by the S&P 500 Index, correctly on six occasions, and it's been wrong six times. So this theory has about as much utility as flipping a coin.

As a snide aside, if any week should have less meaning for the year than the first trading week in January, I can't think of one. Most of the honchos who make the decisions that will really determine how the year will play out don't start showing up at the office until about January 7. Important people just don't work on New Year's Eve, and they like a few days to recuperate from their festivities.

Sell in May and Go Away

Maybe stockbrokers like to take long summer holidays, and thus they use this saying in order to get their clients not to call too often during the summer months. Of course, "sell in May and go away" is more calendar-based bunk that warns that the stock market falls during the summer months. One serious argument put forth in favor of this maxim is that New York City is basically unlivable in the summertime. That fact that the climate is inhospitable promotes some to speculate that the best traders on Wall Street go off on vacation, seeking more temperate zones of comfort and leaving a lot of business to be picked up again in September. This also leaves the impression that the stock market is left in the hands of assistants and recent economics school graduates, who louse things up until better weather brings the Masters of the Universe back to the city. Would that it were true! Retail investors would probably do a lot better for themselves while the sharks are vacationing in Rio.

The truth is, there's nothing about the summer itself that's either good or bad for the market. The Schwab Center for Investment Research examined returns of the S&P 500 Index starting in 1962 and found that, historically, July is actually the best month to invest in stocks. The average July S&P 500 portfolio returns nearly 2 percent. August, returning about 1.5 percent, performed a hair better than November, when the "sell in May and go away" theory says you should be buying. The only historically negative month since 1962 was September, which lost less than 1 percent.

When comparing the periods of May through October to November through April, Schwab found that the May–October months lagged by 0.4 percent. But the center also points out that jumping in and out of the market over such a small number is a bit ludicrous and a sure way to lose money. Where, after all, is your money going to spend the summer? In a cash account averaging a 0.32 percent return? The summer stock market returned 0.8 percent, which is a far more attractive option. Investing year-round is clearly the way to go.

Finally, Schwab looked back to 1926 and charted a $10,000 investment to the present day. If left in the market, the money grew to $23 million. If pulled out of the market every summer and then plowed back in at the first hint of snow, the money grew to only $5.7 million.

All of these calculations leave out some facts that must be considered: Trading stocks costs money, and it generates taxable gains. Active money is the most expensive money you can own. There's one more thing to consider about the Schwab study: It deals in averages. That means there are great Julys and bad Julys. But there's no sure way of knowing which any particular July is going to be until the month actually happens.

Take Profits the Day Before St. Patty's

This myth may be attributable to the luck of the Irish or just the good spirits that tend to linger around the holiday that sometimes (but usually doesn't) heralds spring in New York City. Nevertheless, there are folks out there who believe that the trading day before St. Patrick's Day is a great time to take profits.

Since 1988, however, when March 16 falls on a trading day, the results have been a mixed bag. In 2001, the S&P 500 dropped 23 points before St. Patrick's Day, so taking profits early might have saved investors a bit of pain. The S&P 500 dropped a point in 1999, which would be barely noticeable to investors whether they sold or stayed put. The market was flat on St. Patty's in 1994, so no need to trade there. The S&P 500's largest gain was in 1998, when it rose 11 points for the day. Investors who sold beforehand would have missed out on a bit of a jump. That's not the kind of gain, though, that would have investors shouting with glee in the taverns that night.

All in all, there's just no pattern, which isn't surprising because there's also no logic to this myth. Perhaps a Leprechaun made off with both.

Avoid the October Surprise

The market's fear of October is rooted in the coincidence of historic events. The market dropped precipitously in October in the years 1929, 1937, 1978, 1979, and 1987. October 19, 1987, is still known as Black Monday, when the Dow lost over 500 points, or 22 percent of its value. In the end, that terrible day in 1987 was just a perturbation in the progress of the long bull market that started in 1982 and ended in 2000. Part of the reason that the financial world so persistently remembers 1987's Black Monday is that it harkened back to the October 1929 crash of the stock market that signaled the beginning of the Great Depression.

October has historically been a terrible month for the stock market, but, according to the Schwab Center for Investment Research, September has been worse. That finding makes a bit of sense, because the tradition of avoiding an October surprise calls for selling out of the market in September (the absolute worst investing month of the year). Still, the major market news events have happened, surely by coincidence, in October.

In 1987, the panic in the markets lasted for a day. In 1929, there were many black days. The Dow had climbed from 100 in 1926 to 381 on September 3, 1929. On October 24 (Black Thursday) the market experienced its first major decline, and it continued through the Black Tuesday five days later. During that time, the Dow shed 62 percent of its value over five days, unimpeded by the weekend break.

After 1987's Black Monday, the media was abuzz with talk about a "new Great Depression." Folks on all sides of the issue debated the possibility or likelihood of such an event. Since Black Monday also had a global effect and markets around the world lost money, there was real fear of a global recession or depression on the horizon. One bit of news that might have sparked the rapid decline in stock prices was Brazil's announcement that it would stop making interest payments on its debt, which caused the U.S. dollar to slide. Economists were spooked by the possibility of a contagion: Brazil halts interest payments and the resultant slide in the U.S. dollar causes a recession there, dampening the country's exports and diminishing its need for imports. Some even feared that the United States wanted the U.S. dollar to fall, and fall fast, in order to close its trade deficit. The slowdown in U.S. demands for imported goods might have caused recessions throughout the world, creating an unmanageable financial situation.

That gloomy forecast didn't happen, probably because people knew that that outcome was a possibility. Central banks throughout the world were able to keep money flowing, and the global economy survived. But it was a tense October, not quickly forgotten.

The stock market can crash at any time, of course, whether in reaction to world events or to correct rampant overvaluations. The technology boom really ended in March 2000, a far cry from the month of October. No month is safe, and no month is deadly. Even poor September, the only month that offers negative returns, on average, has its good times.

Aside from that night when the dead walk the Earth, there's no reason to be frightened of October.

There's Always a Santa Claus Rally

The stock market represents the state of our commerce-based economy, and the holidays are, to the lament of many, the most commercialized time of the year. That alone should help the markets.

The Santa Claus rally is a confusing bit of lore. In one formulation it predicts that there will be a bounce in the stock market during the last five trading days of December or the first two trading days of January. If Santa fails to appear, legend has it that stock prices will be lower later in the next year, though the myth doesn't get any more specific than that. In the business media, you will find references to the Santa Claus rally falling anywhere between November and December. So just exactly what this myth says, and its utility for stock traders, is a bit unclear. Mostly, it just seems to stem from folks on Wall Street and the folks who cover Wall Street making folksy holiday references around the holidays.

The Santa Claus rally is also at odds with other bits of investing mythology. There's one myth, for example, that calls for a December slump as investors sell shares in order to take tax losses. That myth feeds into the myth of the January effect, which says that sideline money moves back into the market, often into small-cap stocks, at the start of the year.

One argument in favor of these end-of-year rallies that are attributable to the suit from the North Pole is that some sectors of the economy, particularly in retail and consumer products manufacturing, rely on fourth-quarter earnings to make their years. The time after Thanksgiving is the biggest shopping season in America, after all. But, holiday sales data is sketchy at best in real time, as analysts scramble to measure things like mall traffic and Web site hits in an attempt to divine a bottom line that won't be reported until the early months of the new year.

The Schwab Center for Investment Research gives some credence to the myth, marking December as the third best performing month of the year since 1926, following January by a hair and July. November is the fourth best performing month of the year. So historically, the November–January period has been a good time to hold stocks. But remember that these are average returns, all hovering at about 1.5 percent. No real month is an average month, and returns could well turn negative.

In the end, the market doesn't care about holidays or about the calendar. It's best not to anthropomorphize the market at all.

In the end, the Santa Claus rally is more of a description than a prediction and not something worthwhile on which to trade.

6

People Believe This Stuff?

IT GETS WEIRD. Struggling for some insight into the inner workings of the market, investors have latched onto some loony notions. It's unlikely that anyone uttering these snake oil pitches expects to be taken seriously. But, you never know, and they are fun.

The Super Bowl Theory

Why not mix up stocks and sports? Or investing and gambling? The Super Bowl theory doesn't claim to have a reason for actually existing, it only claims its track record. It says that when teams from the American Football Conference (AFC) win the Super Bowl, the market will finish down for the year, while team victories from the National Football Conference (NFC) will herald positive returns. It's a stupid myth, but people believe it.

One reason this notion might be popular is that the Super Bowl takes place in January. That makes this the fourth January-oriented myth in the book. Clearly, we start each year wondering what the next months will bring and that curiosity seems to express itself in many forms. This theory probably has more to do with January than it does football.

Stocks rose more than 20 percent in 1998 and 1999, despite the AFC's Denver Broncos winning the Bowl those years. But the theory had been correct in predicting S&P 500 returns 28 out of 32 times despite the Bronco's championship run. It led some traders to add "The Elway" exception to the Super Bowl theory, in honor of Bronco's quarterback John Elway.

One reason the theory works is that the AFC isn't as good as the NFC, and the market tends to finish up on a year-over-year basis. If the creator of this theory had been an AFC fan and worked it out so that NFC victories meant bad years for stocks, then the theory never would have had the benefit of coincidence it needed to gain acceptance.

The Markets Fall When the Mets
Win the World Series

Ah, the shame of being the number-two team in New York City. If Yankees World Series wins coincided with bad stock markets, no one would dare speak of Bronx Bombs dropped on the stock market. The Yanks are winners, after all, and thus blameless. But the Mets . . .

When the Mets enjoyed their miracle World Series win in 1969, the Dow fell 15 percent. In victory, the Mets took the blame for the market. When they won in 1986, the market was unfazed. But still, the rumor that the Mets are bad for the stock market persists.

Unfortunately, that's all the data that's available, because the Mets are, though you have got to love them, losers. Here's a myth not worth worrying about, if only because the Mets so seldom win. In the Super Bowl theory the unlikely event of an AFC team winning the Super Bowl seems to explain, in an albeit loopy way, why the stock market usually offers positive returns. This time, it seems like plain old hatred of the team from Queens, who haven't won the big game often enough to establish a pattern either way.

When was the last time they made the series? In 2001, where they lost in four games straight to—the Yankees. The Mets being vanquished by their brethren in the Bronx didn't help the markets any, though, as the S&P 500 lost 9 percent.

The Market Falls When a Horse Wins the Triple Crown

Looks like, in the midst of a recovery, the stock market dodged the bullet when Funny Cide failed in its bid to win the Triple Crown in 2003. To win the Triple Crown, a horse with a jockey on top has to win three major races: The Kentucky Derby, the Belmont Stakes, and the Preakness. I don't know, I don't care much about or for horse racing, but I am pretty sure that this myth is nonsense.

For one thing, the market seems to have no trouble sliding when horses don't win the Triple Crown. A horse hasn't accomplished this feat since 1978, and yet the market still dropped in 2000, 2001, and 2002.

To humor this notion: Out of 10 Triple Crown winners since 1929, the market has fallen eight times. The horses all have funny names. The first was Sir Barton in 1919. The most recent was Affirmed in 1978. The strangest name of all was in 1973—Secretariat. A horse that could type, it seems.

If I'm not taking this one seriously enough, it's because I'm not.

The Cocktail Shrimp Theory:
Big Shrimp Means Big Returns

The logic with this myth is that restaurants, flush with money because of the flood of stock-rich customers, can start serving bigger shrimp in their appetizers, indicating good times in the market and more to come.

Though it hardly needs saying, the size of shrimp has nothing to do with stock performance. Shrimp grow when the water temperature is warm, the algae and plankton they eat is plentiful, and when they don't get scooped up in giant nets before they reach maturity. According to the Louisiana Department of Wildlife and Fisheries, shrimp size has been in decline since the 1970s because the little suckers keep getting caught while they are young.

So enjoy your shrimp—dip it in cocktail sauce or have it sautéed in oil and served over pasta—but don't get your stock market advice from a creature that's basically a seafaring insect with a nerve ganglia instead of a brain. On the other hand, shrimp are at least not clever enough to foist overly optimistic research on you in an attempt to score investment banking–related bonuses.

Short Skirts: Higher Hemlines Mean a Higher Market

Walk onto the floor of the New York Stock Exchange and you will see that most of the traders are still men and that a locker room atmosphere is still in full effect. So it's no surprise that Wall Street would associate higher hemlines with good economic times. A good stock market tends to fill everyone's head with utopian visions. So maybe some folks believe that rollicking economic times means rollicking times all over and that scantily clad women will tromp through the cities in flimsy garments with money flowing out of their purses, but this is a little silly, isn't it?

Recent history proves that this myth is as inane as it sounds. Consider the 1990s, which was the decade of casual dress. While the market more than doubled over the course of the decade, women frequently showed up to work in—pants. The truth is that people wear whatever they want, whenever they want to wear it, and nobody who doesn't need psychological help checks the stock ticker for help in selecting garments out of the closet.

The markets ended a long period of downward and sideways movement in the 1950s, hardly revered as a decade of sexual liberation or a good time for flesh spotting. The markets did advance in the 1960s, the decade of the miniskirt, but the seventies were also a wild time full of flimsy outfits and wanton sexuality and the market didn't react well at all.

In the end, there's only one segment of the market that cares about hemlines—clothiers and retailers—and they don't care how short the skirts are so long as they need to be frequently replaced.

Too bad about this one, though. Were it true, Alan Greenspan might be in charge of raising and lowering hemlines every six weeks. Now *that* would be a news event.

P A **7** R T

The Economy
and Politics

THERE'S NO DOUBT that politics and economics are intertwined. A stubborn recession cost George Herbert Walker Bush the White House, and an economic boom gave two terms to William Jefferson Clinton. Vast amounts of legislation from Washington, D.C., and 50 state capitals attempt to affect the national and local economies every season. As usual, though the connection between politics and the economy is a subject about which few people debate, the practical application of that fact is more difficult to figure out.

The Market Will Collapse When the Baby Boomers Retire

There's a trillion dollars worth of retirement money in the market right now, and someday folks are going to need to cash in their stocks to meet living expenses. The idea of a trillion dollars leaving the market in a whoosh is a pretty scary notion.

This hasn't happened yet, of course, and the good news is that you can bet that it won't. Folks who want to sell alternative investments or to give advice on investing outside of the stock market often make the argument. One such guru is best-selling author Robert Kiyosaki, who wrote a book called *Rich Dad's Prophecy*. In that work he advances the argument that the biggest stock market crash in history is looming on the horizon and that to guard against it people should take their money out of the stock market and invest in tangibles like real estate. By the way, Mr. Kiyosaki also has other products like compact discs, videotapes, and seminar tickets for sale that will aid you in that endeavor.

Kiyosaki makes a demographic argument for the impending stock market disaster. The baby boomers have most of their retirement money in the stock market through mutual funds and 401(k) programs. When they retire, they will start drawing on that money for their living expenses; the market will collapse because the smaller generation following in the boomer wake won't be putting enough money into the market to keep the ship afloat. It's basically the Social Security problem transferred to the stock market.

But, while the Social Security system is in trouble, the stock market isn't. Remember that the baby boomers are defined as folks born between 1946 and 1964. So 77 million people aren't all going to retire on the same day.

Also staving off any day of doom is the fact that lifespans are increasing. Scenario planner Peter Schwartz believes that by the year 2020 most Americans will be taking some form of age-slowing therapy from their doctors. The fact is, a good percentage of the current population, including a lot of the baby boomers, is going to work longer than expected. Even without advances in medical technology, the average U.S. citizen has a 50/50 chance of living into his or her middle nineties. All of this means that the years of retirement for the baby boomers will be wider than the naysayers plan. Though their money will eventually flow out of the market, the transition will be orderly (managed over years, if not decades) and won't cause a crash.

Kiyosaki also overstates the effect of boomer investments, particularly through mutual funds, on the market. The biggest buyers and sellers of securities haven't been individual investors in aggregate, they have been corporations who buy up their own stock in share buyback programs (something they have to do as they issue diluting stock options and restricted stock to executives) or for their own portfolios.

According to Andrew Smithers and Stephen Wright, corporations, rather than institutions or individuals, were the net buyers of common stock throughout most of the 1990s, which means, in the very least, that the market is simply not a proxy for baby boomer retirement money.

The Stock Market Is a Leading
Economic Indicator

A leading indicator is any measurable part of the economy that might provide some insight as to where the economy at large is headed. The stock market, being so easily measured by the price of its constituent securities, is a favorite leading indicator among the popular media. It is also, unlike other data such as new-car sales, housing starts, consumer confidence, and jobless claims, updated daily, which feeds our need to constantly know what the economy is going to be like a year from now. It's also rather hard to ignore that the stock market crash of 1929 did presage the Great Depression. Unfortunately, the belief that stock market performance today will determine the economy tomorrow is a dangerous notion for investors who might get spooked by large daily or weekly market declines.

The stock market is actually a rotten leading indicator. Consider the 1970s, when the stock market suffered massive losses in the face of rising inflation caused by the OPEC oil embargo. In that case, the market lagged oil prices. It can also be argued that incredibly cheap oil throughout the 1990s helped to fuel the stock market's rise throughout that decade.

The 1990s were also fueled by an accommodative monetary policy from the Federal Reserve, which the bank halted and reversed in the latter part of the decade, which helped to cause the burst of the technology bubble. The loss of trillions of dollars of stock and bond wealth during that period certainly hurt the economy going forward. But if Alan Greenspan is right, it was the economy that punctured the markets, not the markets that punctured the economy.

Remember also that after the technology-fueled boom fizzled, pundits predicted many more dire scenarios for the U.S. economy than actually came about. Before the country even experienced a mild recession by historical standards, folks were talking about double-dip recessions, double-digit unemployment, and even the possibility of deflation. Most of the horror was to have been caused by a contraction of the wealth effect when the once-stock-rich realized they were now stock poor and stopped spending money.

In the end, even despite the devastating terrorist attacks on New York City and Washington, D.C., the economy was able to hobble along as the Federal Reserve cut interest rates and sparked a boom in the housing and mortgage refinancing markets. Low interest rates also allowed auto manufacturers to offer 0 percent financing on new-car purchases, and so consumers spent money in spite of the stock market's losses. In this case, the Fed and U.S. industry combined to show that they could react to bad stock performance in a way that would keep the economy afloat.

The stock market does, of course, represent the sum total of investors' expectations about the future, so a collapse in the market means that there is negative sentiment at play. But sentiment doesn't determine reality; it is a reaction based on the perception of reality at a given time.

A proper leading indicator should, in most cases, predict the future, and the stock market fails that test. That's great news for investors who learned in 1987 that the country can weather a stock market shock and still grow. So there's no need to panic when the market heads south, because it doesn't mean long lines at the soup kitchen anymore.

Tax Cuts End Recessions

A recession is defined as a contraction in the gross domestic product of the United States for at least two quarters, meaning that businesses are, on average, selling less of their products and services than they used to. A favorite tactic among politicians from both political parties is to try and stimulate the economy by lowering taxes. (John F. Kennedy and Ronald Reagan, to name two opposing sides of the political spectrum, both did so.) They cut taxes in hopes of putting more money in consumers' wallets, which they intend to then hand over to the business community. Recessions are terrible for the stock market, which is driven by earnings growth. A good portion of the investment community believes that tax cuts end recessions, thus aiding the market. The truth lies, of course, right in the middle. Some tax cuts end recessions. Others have little or no effect.

One reason that a tax cut doesn't signal a moment to jump into the market with the expectation of better times ahead is that the effect of a tax cut might not be felt for years. (Most budget bills reach out 10 years into the future, when the president pushing them will be out of office and possibly working on his memoirs.) By that time, major news events that have come after the tax cut could mute the significance of the legislation. One recent case in point: George W. Bush's tax rebate during his first summer in office had its economic effect squashed by the September 11 terrorist attacks.

One argument that makes a lot of sense is that recessions can be ended by tax cuts, but only if it's the right kind of tax cut. Michael A. Meeropol of the Economic Policy Institute examined two recessions and two tax cuts to illustrate this point. First, Meeropol looked at the 1974–1975 recession that was presided over by President Gerald Ford. This was a bad recession, with unemployment rising from 4.8 percent to 8.9 percent in a matter of months and gross domestic product dropping at 3.8 percent per year. Ford tried to end the recession by spurring consumer spending. He enacted the Earned Income Tax Credit (EITC) that allows low-income Americans to pay no federal tax at all. He offered a $100 (in today's dollars) credit for all tax-payers and their dependents, and he increased the standard deduction. He left marginal tax rates alone. It worked as a spending stimulus. Consumer spending as a percentage of GDP rose from 61.7 percent to 63.1 percent and remained at that higher level throughout the 1970s. But it didn't help the stock market. People spent their new cash, they didn't invest it. Now, that eventually helps the markets because it increases corporate income and thus stock values, but it didn't have a quick-fix stimulative effect on stocks.

Still, GDP started growing again by the second quarter of 1975, and the unemployment rate started dropping.

In the fourth quarter of 1981, we were back in a recession again, but under a new president. Ronald Reagan relied on an already-passed trickle-down tax cut for wealthy Americans and corporations as unemployment approached 11 percent. Though the 1981 recession lasted about as long as the recession under Ford, it was much more severe. Consumer spending didn't grow, unemployment was much higher, and the federal budget deficit grew out of hand as the tax cuts deprived the government of resources while failing to stimulate consumer spending or other economic growth.

One key difference between the Ford and Reagan plans (aside from the beneficiaries of the tax cut) is that Ford's cut was immediate while most of Reagan's cuts were phased in over the course of the recession. A recession always demands some immediate action or it will grow out of control.

There is some debate in modern times, when the top tax bracket is about 35 percent (it was once over 70 percent), about whether or not tax cutting has lost some of its stimulative power. If it has, then perhaps government spending will become the recession-fighting tool of choice. It worked for President Franklin Roosevelt during the Great Depression when he put Americans to work as part of his Works Projects Administration and then as part of the burgeoning war effort.

All Wars Feed Bulls

This little saying should make all stock investors so bloodthirsty that they should be constantly writing to Congress to demand attacks on whatever rogue nation has captured the limelight for the moment. If there were really money to be made, ordinary folks would behave that way. At this point, it's still reasonable to believe that certain members of the defense industry, or what President Eisenhower once dubbed "the military-industrial complex," do lobby for violence across international borders. But the myth that war helps the common investor is really just a giant historic misunderstanding.

In the big picture, wars are bad for the economy, and bad economies make for bad stock markets. The first income tax levied on U.S. citizens followed the Civil War. Burdened by enormous war debts, the government had little choice but to implement the unpopular tax. If the Revolutionary War was a battle against taxation, then the Civil War was the battle that brought it back, and that's why companies like Tyco like to set up their corporate status in the Bahamas.

Now, it is an old truism of history class that World War II and the vast mobilization of industry that went with it shook the last vestiges of the Great Depression off a stagnant U.S. economy. But those were different times. World War II lasted six years, and the United States fought through four of those. General Motors stopped churning out so many cars and started manufacturing tanks and halftracks. The Ford Motor Company produced a great deal of airplane engines. Women flooded into the workplace as men were called into military service. How's that for a jump in productivity? American industry found an entirely unexploited source of new labor.

Fortunately, the United States has never again had to confront a war as terrible in scope and ferocity as World War II. In the long term, the economy and the stock market just don't react to a week of fighting for medical students in Grenada or to the invasion of Panama to a Guns and Roses soundtrack. Remember the first Gulf War and how it failed to save the presidency of George Herbert Walker Bush? After the dust had settled in that month-long war, the economy emerged in the same place it had begun—as an economy about to use productivity gains and new technologies to recover from a recession.

Between January 2003 through the end of April of the same year the United States prepared for and fought the second Gulf War. Though the markets had volatile days and sometimes traded on war news, a tangible recovery didn't occur until months after the war ended. It could be argued that the uncertainty about the war and how it would go actually stalled a recovery that might have taken place months earlier in a time of peace. During the brief war, nothing changed for the American economy. Unemployment, at about 5.8 percent at the beginning of the year, was at 6.1 percent at the end of the war. The Federal Reserve held interest rates firm at 1.25 percent. Ford unveiled a new Mustang sports car, not the engine for a new fighter jet.

The only reason that World War II set the stage for an economic recovery was that it completely engulfed and remade the culture of the country. No skirmish will do that, and no one wants another world war.

8

A Few
Misunderstandings

NOT QUITE MYTHS but common beliefs, the following chapters explore some general investing notions that every investor will eventually have to confront.

Your Investments Are Insured

Very few investments are actually insured by the government. If you have a corporate pension plan, your company is required to insure those benefits in case you outlive the company. If you have a bank account, the Federal Deposit Insurance Corporation insures you against losses up to $100,000 in the case of a bank failure. But really, the list of insured investments is rather meager.

Money in a brokerage account is not federally insured. Though most people believe that the government would step in to prevent the collapse of Ginnie Mae or Freddie Mac (once federal agencies, now public companies), the government is not required by law to do so. Owning the bonds of or stock in Ginnie Mae and Freddie Mac is, to the government's eye, the same as owning stock in Microsoft. One could reason that the government stepped in to bail out savings and loans businesses during the 1980s when it had no obligation to do so. But there is some risk involved in that belief, because government policies are as difficult to predict as the stock market.

The Federal Deposit Insurance Corporation lists all insured investment vehicles on its Web site at www.fdic.gov. If an investment isn't on that list, assume the government does not insure it.

According to the FDIC, the following investment items are insured:

Traditional bank accounts, including checking, savings, trusts (excluding any securities held by the trust), certificates of deposit, and money market accounts are all insured up to $100,000.

That's it. The FDIC specifically lists the following as not insured:

Mutual funds, common stock, bonds, or shares in a limited partnership. The contents of safe deposit boxes are also not insured by the government nor, the FDIC notes, are they generally insured by the bank. It's up to the consumer to buy fire or theft insurance for items left in a safe deposit vault.

One bit of good news is that any securities investment kept in the custody of a brokerage house is insured against physical loss by the Securities Investor Protection Corporation, which provides up to $500,000 in protection for securities and $100,000 for cash in a broker's custody. So if a brokerage house fails, an investor isn't entirely out of luck.

Treasury securities are not insured by the FDIC in the event of a bank failure. But the FDIC points out that the bank is usually just the custodian of those bonds and that records are kept so that an investor will retain ownership should the bank collapse.

CDs Are Safe

A CD, or certificate of deposit, is basically a high-yield bank account with restrictions on when you can withdraw your money. They are believed to be safe investments because they are considered to be safe investments. The money is as safe as the money in a normal savings or checking account, and the first $100,000 is insured against bank failure by the Federal Deposit Insurance Corporation. But the term "safe" is relative. You won't lose principle in a CD, but that doesn't mean you can't lose ground against the rest of the economy.

One reason that money should be invested, rather than stowed in a fireproof filing cabinet in the toolshed, is that inflation eats into the purchasing power of any dollar. Interest paid on CDs, money market accounts, and bank accounts fluctuates and often won't keep up with inflation in the long term.

Money market accounts are similar to CDs except that they are short term and generally allow for immediate withdrawal. They pay better than most bank savings accounts but not so well as CDs, and they are insured. Money market mutual funds, which are administered by a fund company that invests money in various money markets, seeking the best return, are not bank accounts and thus are not insured. That said, they are generally safe funds, and no reputable money market mutual fund has ever lost money for investors. The only real risk is, of course, that the money won't keep up with inflation. The money market mutual fund investor benefits from having a manager seek out the best possible returns, but the fund also has to beat both inflation and the annual management fee.

Another option for investors seeking a place to park cash is to buy short-term Treasury bills from the U.S. government, which generally mature between three and five years and are sometimes indexed to inflation. Longer-term notes are also available. These are backed by the U.S. government, so default, while not an impossibility, is virtually impossible. Though these bonds are liquid and traded frequently on the open market, the best prices aren't always available so there's some risk involved for investors who find themselves needing their cash quickly.

While all of these investments are basically safe for the principal invested, the stock market has offered superior returns, when given enough time. Cash investments like CDs, money market funds, and Treasuries should be used for money that absolutely must be preserved or kept for ready or near-term access.

You Should Take Advantage of Tax-Free Accounts

The government offers a few options for investors planning for retirements and for college tuition savings that can cut down on the tax bill. The three basic types are the 401(k) plan, the IRA, and the state-government-administered 529 College Savings Plan.

The first, and easiest to use, is the 401(k) retirement plan offered by most companies. These plans are usually administered by an outside investment advisory firm like Fidelity or Merrill Lynch. Though the individual plans differ from company to company, they usually offer an array of stock, bond, and cash mutual funds from which investors can choose. Investor money is taken right out of the paycheck, before federal and state taxes are removed, so participation in the plan has immediate tax benefits. Once in the plan, the money is allowed to grow, free of taxes, which aren't paid until an investor retires and begins taking distributions from the account. Often, companies will match employee contributions to the plan, though they aren't required by law to do so. Employees can invest either $12,000 a year or 10 percent of their salaries, whichever is less. The maximum amount will increase to $15,000 in 2006.

The money isn't available until retirement, though it can be rolled over into a new plan, if an employee switches jobs. Investors can also borrow against 401(k) accounts at a favorable rate of interest that generally falls within the 6 to 8 percent that they could expect from the stock market in the long term. One risk with borrowing is that if an employee switches jobs with a loan outstanding and a new 401(k) plan won't allow for a rollover of the loan, the full amount may be due immediately. Failure to pay the loan back counts as an "early distribution" from the plan and will be subject to a 10 percent penalty in addition to income taxes. Still, the 401(k) plan is an easy and tax-efficient way to invest, and it's good to take advantage of them.

Companies that match employee contributions to the plan will generally do so only to a certain percentage of the employee's salary. If a company will match up to 5 percent, for example, it's a good idea to invest at least 5 percent a year. To invest less would basically be to turn down free money from the boss.

An Individual Retirement Account, or IRA, is a good alternative for people without access to 401(k) plans or who need to save additional money for retirement. An IRA generally works like a 401(k) account in that money is allowed to grow tax-free, but the maximum annual contribution is usually just $3000. Depending on the income level of the investor, IRA contributions might be tax deductible. In the Roth IRA, created as part of the 1997 tax bill, contributions are never tax deductible but distributions from the plan, taken after the investor is 59½ years old, are not subject to any tax. Unlike the 401(k) plans, distributions from these accounts can't occur without penalty until the investor is age 59½, and distributions must begin when the investor is age 70½.

A 529 College Savings Plan is a state-run investment vehicle that generally allows money to grow through mutual funds, on a tax-deferred basis, so long as the money is used to pay the qualified tuition expenses of a student in college. Although rules vary from state to state, contributions to these accounts are generally deductible from both state and federal income taxes. Because the account is in the name of the student (generally a low-wage earner) and not the investor who sets it up, taxes on the money, once withdrawn, are lower.

Though most states offer these plans, there's no requirement that investors use their home state's 529 Plan. It's important to shop around, as most plans have a program management fee of about 1 percent in addition to the underlying fees of the mutual funds that are the ultimate investment vehicles. One drawback to buying out of state is that contributions might not be deductible from the taxes your state charges its residents. On the other hand, if another state offers a lower-fee program or better mutual funds, it might be worth losing the state tax deduction. Investors in states with no income tax should feel free to shop around. The federal tax deduction applies to all plans.

A few drawbacks to the 529 Plan is that the money is basically lost. Since the beneficiary of the account is the student, there's no way for an investor to withdraw money in the case of an emergency. The investor generally cedes all decision making to the program manager. Some programs offer preset alternatives, where money starts in stocks and moves to safer instruments as the beneficiary reaches college age. Others offer portfolios ranging from aggressive to conservative. Generally, an investor won't be able to switch from one state's program to another or to switch investment styles once papers have been signed. Finally, these plans don't guarantee principle, nor do they guarantee to keep up with rising tuition costs. Still, if you are going to save for college, this is the best way.

There's not much free out there for investors, but you shouldn't pass up on these three government-sanctioned investment accounts.

Sophisticated Investors Are in Hedge Funds

Hedge fund managers were the investment celebrities of the roaring 1990s. George Soros of the Quantum Fund and Julian Robertson of the Tiger Fund became household names. Robertson was a value investor while Soros delved into the world of "global macro" investing and made large bets on local currencies.

Since about 1990, hedge funds have been considered the vehicles to own. Part of that appeal is the glamour. The SEC only lets wealthy people invest in hedge funds, and while mutual fund managers take whatever money's sent, hedge fund managers often choose their investors. The exclusivity alone was enough to make ordinary investors want to play. The SEC's definition of wealthy isn't really that exclusive as it includes anyone with an annual salary of over $200,000 a year or investable assets of $1 million (and the house counts). Investors who never thought they'd have the opportunity might well find themselves tempted by the hedge fund world. In 2000, the industry had raised about $500 billion worldwide, up from just $15 billion in 1990. Celebrity investors included Barbra Streisand, Senator Robert Torricelli, and Bianca Jagger.

Any industry that contains styles as different as Robertson and Soros will be difficult to define. The truth is, the phrase "hedge fund" has very little meaning anymore. As defined by Alfred Winslow Jones in 1949, a hedge fund invests both long and short in equities, hoping that the long positions would be up while the market climbed and that the short positions would cushion the blow of a market tumble. Managers have tried, without success, to figure out the perfect hedge, a portfolio that's up consistently no matter what the market's doing.

But a good number of hedge funds don't hedge at all. Some invest in currencies, some invest in mortgage-backed securities, some seek to arbitrage bond yields through short-term trades, and some make large investments in small public companies, hoping to rehabilitate them and then to sell them to larger rivals. The universe of hedge funds has grown so broad that many financial planners prefer to call them "alternative investment vehicles."

All of them charge high fees. The expense ratio is between 1 percent and 2 percent of assets, but the managers will also take between 20 and 25 percent of the profits made that year. They also tend to be illiquid. Managers might demand that money invested can't be taken out for between one and five years. They might also say that, after the lock-up has passed, money can only be withdrawn with a three-month notice. Managers argue that they can't properly execute their strategies with money flowing in and out like a mutual fund. Some hedge fund managers have superb pedigrees, but anyone who hasn't been permanently barred from the securities industry by the SEC can open a hedge fund. Even those who have been barred can open a hedge fund overseas and sell to investors outside of the United States. John Meriwether, a partner of the failed Long Term Capital Management, is still in the business, and Joseph Jett, once fined $200,000 by the Securities and Exchange Commission and forced to return $8 million in profits made as a mortgage bond trader from Kidder Peabody, has a fund too.

Disclosure is also sometimes scant. The manager might send a quarterly statement but is not required to give anything more than a general picture of how the fund has been managed. Though the SEC can prosecute a hedge fund manager for fraud or for violating securities laws, the hedge fund industry in the U.S. is basically unregulated.

Technically, it's not even quite right to refer to investors and managers in this case. Hedge funds are limited partnerships and the manager, as the general partner, holds all of the power.

Usually, hedge funds have a high minimum investment requirement, over $1 million. But some smaller funds will settle for $10,000. Most managers have written into their charters that they can reduce the minimum investment requirement on a case-by-case basis. Investors without $1 million to invest can still get into the big hedge funds through a fund of funds, which is a fund that pools money to invest in hedge funds. That structure adds yet another layer of fees.

Of course, the fees might not matter so much if hedge funds can deliver outsized returns. But the funds have to overcome their fees to do it. Vanguard founder John Bogle, the investment community's foremost enemy of high-fee investments, has estimated that a fund with a 2 percent expense ratio and an agreement to hand 20 percent of profits to the manager would have to show a 17 percent return to beat the market in a year when the market's up 17 percent. Certainly, a 17 percent year is possible. But it's just not likely that a manager will be able to repeat such a feat over the long term, and most fund managers want investors' money for awhile.

The SEC Keeps Average Investors Out of Risky Investments

We are lucky to have the SEC, which has proven to be a vigilant watchdog against fraud and corruption in the stock market and the investment world at large since 1934. The agency has certainly done its part in helping the United States develop a liquid and efficient stock market. But don't feel too secure. The SEC is only an enforcement agency, after all, and the laws are written by Congress. Some of those laws have been left to languish for a while. So the SEC's determination of what makes a "sophisticated" investor sets the bar pretty low.

There are two classes of investments out there. One represents the stocks, bonds, and cash investments that are most commonly discussed and are available to the general public through a variety of means. Another includes limited partnerships in real estate, oil wells, offshore rigs, private companies, venture capital funds, private equity funds, hedge funds, and a myriad of other vehicles. (It seems like there is a new one every day.) This second type is supposed to be reserved for qualified investors, defined as sophisticated by the SEC. Though circumstances vary from program to program, most of these exclusive investments aren't regulated by the government. Quarterly and annual reports aren't filed. The SEC can pursue fraud charges against managers, but these investment programs generally act outside of the government's purview.

A sophisticated investor, under the current law, is defined as having either income of $200,000 a year or an investable net worth of $1 million. Though these folks are certainly wealthier than the average investor, a diligent investment program combined with a robust professional life could catapult a lot of people to this level by the time they are approaching retirement age. The value of a home, for example, counts toward the calculation of investable net worth. Though a sophisticated investor does have a good deal of money, it's fairly easy to slide from affluence. The United States and Canada lost 100,000 millionaires between 2001 and 2002, according to a study by Merrill Lynch and Cap Gemini Ernst & Young. The total net worth of millionaires in the United States and Canada dropped $200 billion as well. Staying rich can be as difficult as getting rich. And with a whole new slew of investment options suddenly available, financial planning becomes ever more complicated.

A lot of these investments cater to the superwealthy or to institutions. These investments will generally require minimum investments of between $5 and $10 million, and the money will be locked away for a while. Venture capital firms and private equity funds often operate this way. But there are a lot of smaller operations out there that want to take money from individuals and have lower minimums, between $10,000 and $100,000. They tend to be set up as limited partnerships meaning that the manager of the program is a general partner (given full authority to administer funds and run the program) and that the investor is a limited partner. While a mutual fund investor can vote for board members or even vote to remove the current management team, the limited partner usually has little or no voting rights. The general partner is, well, the general of the field and not subject to question of input from the limited partners.

For big-money institutions, limited partner status isn't a problem. The fact that they have billions of dollars to invest gives them substantial influence over the general partners that need their money. Individual investors can't play the billion-dollar portfolio card. It's fair to be suspicious of venture capital private equity and hedge funds that solicit individual investors through brokers and salespeople. If these managers were good enough to raise big-money investments from the major retirement funds and investment banks, they would probably do that. Generally, part of the sales pitch from these funds will be that they are offering to the individual what was once only available to major institutions. But what the institutions demand are transparency and quality management. If an investment is being sold as a cold call or at a cheesy conference in a hotel lobby, it probably won't pass institutional muster.

Fraud is rampant in this world. The most common scheme is the Ponzi, named after Boston financier Charles Ponzi, who picked up on an old con and formed a company called The Securities and Exchange Company. (This happened before the days of the SEC we now know and love.) Ponzi sold stakes in his company and promised a 50 percent return within 45 days. Of course, the business did nothing. So Ponzi used money from new investors to pay his old investors and hoped the whole thing wouldn't fall apart, as it inevitably did. Though the scheme of using new money to pay old obligations has been named after him, Ponzi didn't invent the scheme. It was around before him and is still around today.

For the rich who are private banking clients at places like JPMorgan Chase, FleetBoston, or Citigroup (any reputable bank, really), such opportunities are vetted by professionals who represent major institutions with money to spend. Most people don't have $5 million accounts that merit such personal treatment. But if a cold call or investment conference opportunity looks compelling, be sure to mention it to a financial adviser at one of the larger institutions. They will be able to see, by making a few calls, if their company has ever heard of the opportunity. If they haven't, let it go. That means the bank isn't putting its best clients into the program.

One other way for investors to check out such opportunities is to type the name of everyone involved into the Google search engine and to query the National Association of Securities Dealers, which will provide records on partnership managers' previous brokerage work in the securities industry. Beware, though. Not all thieves have stolen before, or have been caught, so their names might not show up during a search for shady characters.

The unregulated investment world is alluring, but step into it lightly. Its complexities can make the stock market seem simple.

The Higher the Risk, the Higher the Return

Some investors thrive on risk, and some learn to thrive on risk because they have been told over and over again that low-risk investments tend to deliver lower returns. It even makes sense to look at the act of investing as an attempt to collect compensation for risk endured. What's important, then, is for investors to make sure that the compensation they want to collect is adequate to the risk involved in an investment.

Take a simple investment like a bank account. The risk is so miniscule that we tend to assume it's not even there. Since all accounts under $100,000 are insured by the Federal Deposit Insurance Corporation, the bank would have to fail and a government agency would have to collapse before a saver would lose money on most bank account investments. Still, the banks do pay for the money, generally at a paltry rate below 2 percent a year.

Risk is especially well codified in the corporate bond market. Companies that merit strong ratings by Standard & Poor's or Moody's don't have to pay high interest to bondholders in order to borrow cash. A good company might pay between 3 and 5 percent interest to its bondholders. A company with a less favorable rating that's borrowing money to keep from going under and that faces an uncertain future might have to pay between 10 and 15 percent to its bondholders. (These types of investments are known as high-yield or junk bonds.) The greater the risk, say bondholders, the better the compensation they demand—and they want it in writing.

Stock investors get very little in writing when they buy their shares. The price, set daily, is the price. Bond prices fluctuate but as long as a company remains solvent and doesn't miss its interest payments, a bondholder can always hang on to the debt until it matures and then cash out with what was promised. A stockholder is promised nothing.

In that sense, the stock market is riskier than the bond market in general and should always provide superior returns. But it isn't so. While the total stock market declined 14 percent between 2000 and the end of 2002, the Lehman Brothers Long-Term Treasury Index was up 14 percent. We're talking long-term Treasuries here, as vanilla a type of bond as you will ever find. During those years, safe bonds paid more than risky stocks.

All this means, of course, is that risk and higher returns don't always walk hand in hand. If we adjust the myth a bit and say that riskier investments promise higher returns, we are getting closer to the truth and we have a myth that's best used backwards. Whenever investors hear a high-return promise, they should immediately wonder about the risks involved.

One way to mitigate risk in the stock market, where shareholders don't have the benefit of promised returns, is to concentrate on fundamental analysis when stock picking. This option seems to avoid the question of a stock's price volatility, and most investors assume that risk and volatility are one and the same. I think that's a misguided notion. Volatility is a symptom of risk, not the cause. If a stock's price is prone to manic-depressive highs and lows, then the market is signaling that it's having a hard time assigning a valuation to the company. The market is reasonably good at assigning valuations, so this phenomenon should reflect on the company: News events might be driving the stock, the stock might be caught up in a fad or mania, or Wall Street might now be questioning the future of the company's industry. Those are some of the events that cause price swings and, thus, volatility. Knowing a company well is the best way to pick stocks that won't be prone to frequent bouts of uncertainty from other traders.

It's best to view investing as a job where you are being paid to assume risk on someone else's behalf. You might really want or need $1000 right now. If I offered you the money to cut my lawn, it might sound like a good deal. And you might take it, because $1000 is a lot of money for grass cutting—unless, of course, I want you to do it with a nonmotorized push mower and my lawn is 1000 acres of tumbleweeds and scrub bush in West Texas. It's your responsibility to ask for the details before you sign the contract.

Earning a return is every investor's goal. But make sure the return is fair, because you will be asked to work for it.

Index

About the Author

Michael Maiello is a staff writer at *Forbes* magazine where he has covered a wide array of topics, usually about Wall Street, since starting there in the fall of 1999. Assignments have taken him to Germany, to the most northern and remote areas of Canada's Northwest Territories, and to Nigeria's Niger Delta. He is also a playwright with shows produced off-off Broadway in New York and around the country. Two of his plays have been published by *Playscripts, Inc.* He has written book reviews for the *San Francisco Chronicle* and the *New York Times Book Review*. Prior to taking his position at *Forbes,* Maiello lived and worked as a journalist in New Mexico, starting his career at age 15 as a sports and news stringer for the *Albuquerque Tribune,* a Scripps Howard afternoon daily.